EDITOR: Maryanne Blacker

FOOD EDITOR: Pamela Clark

∎ ∎ ∎

ART DIRECTOR: Sue de Guingand

∎ ∎ ∎

ASSISTANT FOOD EDITOR: Louise Patniotis

ASSOCIATE FOOD EDITOR: Enid Morrison

SENIOR HOME ECONOMISTS: Kathy McGarry,
Sophia Young

HOME ECONOMISTS: Frances Abdallaoui, Angela
Bresnahan, Karen Buckley, Caroline Jones, Leisel Rogers

EDITORIAL COORDINATOR: Elizabeth Hooper

KITCHEN ASSISTANT: Amy Wong

∎ ∎ ∎

STYLISTS: Marie-Helene Clauzon, Carolyn Fienberg,
Jane Hann, Jacqui Hing, Cherise Koch

PHOTOGRAPHERS: Kevin Brown, Robert Clark,
Robert Taylor, Jon Waddy

∎ ∎ ∎

HOME LIBRARY STAFF:

ASSISTANT EDITOR: Bridget van Tinteren

DESIGNER: Robbylee Phelan

EDITORIAL COORDINATOR: Fiona Lambrou

∎ ∎ ∎

ACP PUBLISHER: Richard Walsh

ACP DEPUTY PUBLISHER: Nick Chan

ACP CIRCULATION & MARKETING DIRECTOR:
Judy Kiernan

∎ ∎ ∎

Produced by The Australian Women's Weekly Home Library.
Typeset by ACP Colour Graphics Pty Ltd.
Colour separations by Network Graphics Pty. Ltd. in Sydney.
Printing by Hannanprint. in Sydney.
Published by ACP Publishing Pty Ltd, 54 Park Street, Sydney.
♦ AUSTRALIA: Distributed by Network Distribution Company,
54 Park Street Sydney, (02) 282 8777.
♦ UNITED KINGDOM: Distributed in the U.K. by Australian
Consolidated Press (UK) Ltd, 20 Galowhill Rd, Brackmills,
Northampton NN4 OEE (0604) 760 456.
♦ CANADA: Distributed in Canada by Whitecap Books Ltd,
351 Lynn Ave, North Vancouver B.C. V7J 2C4 (604) 980 9852.
♦ NEW ZEALAND: Distributed in New Zealand by Netlink
Distribution Company, 17B Hargreaves St, Level 5,
College Hill, Auckland 1 (9) 302 7616.
♦ SOUTH AFRICA: Distributed in South Africa by Intermag,
PO Box 57394, Springfield 2137 (011) 493 3200.

∎ ∎ ∎

Quick Mix Biscuits & Slices

Includes index.
ISBN 1 86396 029 5

1. Cookies. 2. Quick and easy cookery.
I Title: Australian Women's Weekly. (Series:
Australian Women's Weekly Home Library).

641.8654

∎ ∎ ∎

© A C P Publishing Pty Limited 1994
ACN 053 273 546

∎ ∎ ∎

COVER: Clockwise from back: Fruit and Nut Choc Chip
Cookies, page 84, Pistachio Chocolate Biscuits, page 23,
Almond Jam Cookies, page 17.
Cookie jar, jug and butter dish from Home & Garden on the Mall.
OPPOSITE: Anise Marmalade Crescents, page 109.
BACK COVER: Choc Ginger Raisin Slice, Iiage 40.

Quick-Mix Biscuits & Slices

We have made these scrumptious biscuits and slices
using the quickest, easiest methods we know. Many are
mixed in just one bowl, and some are unbaked. For
convenience, different types of confectionery and
packaged biscuits are used in this book; these are
pictured in our extensive glossary so you can readily
identify them. But, first, turn to page 124 for tips on how
to get perfect results every time. An oven temperature
guide is given on page 127.

Pamela Clark

FOOD EDITOR

BRITISH & NORTH AMERICAN READERS: Please note that
Australian cup and spoon measurements are metric. A quick conversion
guide appears on page 127.
A glossary explaining unfamiliar terms and ingredients appears on page 120.

WALNUT CORNMEAL BISCOTTI

125g butter, chopped
1 cup (220g) caster sugar
2 eggs
1 tablespoon walnut oil
1½ cups (225g) plain flour
¾ cup (110g) self-raising flour
½ cup (85g) cornmeal
1¼ cups (125g) walnuts,
toasted, chopped

Beat butter and sugar in medium bowl with electric mixer until smooth. Add eggs and oil, beat until combined. Stir in flours, cornmeal and nuts. Shape mixture into 4 x 3.5cm diameter logs, place about 8cm apart on greased oven trays. Bake in moderately slow oven about 30 minutes or until browned. Lift onto wire racks; cool 10 minutes.

Using a serrated knife, cut logs diagonally into 1cm slices. Place slices, cut side down, on baking paper-covered oven trays. Bake in moderately slow oven about 10 minutes or until browned. Lift biscotti onto wire racks to cool.

Makes about 60.

MARZIPAN NUT PETITS FOURS

½ cup (65g) Butternut Cookie crumbs
¼ cup (60ml) Nutella
2 tablespoons chopped roasted
hazelnuts
30g soft butter
1 tablespoon cocoa
½ x 200g packet marzipan
icing sugar mixture
cocoa, extra

Combine cookie crumbs, Nutella, nuts, butter and cocoa in bowl; mix well. Place mixture onto plastic wrap, shape into 25cm log. Roll marzipan between sheets of baking paper to 11cm x 25cm rectangle. Place log onto marzipan, wrap marzipan around log, smooth join with fingers, cover; refrigerate until firm. Cut log diagonally into 1cm slices. Dust half the slices with sifted icing sugar. Dust remaining slices with extra sifted cocoa.

Makes 25.

ABOVE: Walnut Cornmeal Biscotti.
RIGHT: Marzipan Nut Petits Fours.

ORANGE HAZELNUT CRISPS

100g butter, chopped
⅓ cup (80ml) vegetable oil
2 teaspoons grated orange rind
½ cup (80g) icing sugar mixture
½ cup (110g) caster sugar
1 egg
1½ cups (225g) plain flour
½ cup (75g) self-raising flour
½ cup (60g) finely chopped roasted hazelnuts
¼ teaspoon ground nutmeg

Beat butter, oil, rind, sugars and egg in large bowl with electric mixer until smooth. Stir in remaining ingredients, mix to a soft dough; refrigerate until firm. Roll rounded teaspoons of mixture into balls with floured hands, place about 5cm apart on greased oven trays, flatten to 5mm thick. Bake in moderate oven about 12 minutes or until browned; cool on wire racks.

Makes about 60.

SPICED CHOC NUT PANFORTE

Chopped carob and carob powder can be substituted for dark chocolate and cocoa, if preferred.

15.5cm x 24cm sheet rice paper
½ cup (125ml) honey
½ cup (110g) caster sugar
1 cup (150g) macadamias, toasted, halved
⅓ cup (50g) roasted hazelnuts
⅓ cup (55g) blanched almonds, toasted
⅓ cup (50g) shelled pistachios, toasted
⅓ cup (85g) finely chopped glace apricots
2 tablespoons mixed peel
2 tablespoons finely chopped dried figs
2 tablespoons sultanas
2 teaspoons ground cinnamon
1 teaspoon mixed spice
¼ teaspoon ground cardamom
60g dark chocolate, finely chopped
2 tablespoons cocoa
½ cup (75g) plain flour

Grease 8cm x 26cm bar cake pan, place strip of baking paper to cover base and extend over 2 opposite sides; grease paper. Cut rice paper in half lengthways. Cover base of prepared pan with a piece of the rice paper.

Combine honey and sugar in medium heavy-based pan, stir over low heat, without boiling, until sugar is dissolved. Bring to boil, quickly stir in remaining ingredients; mix well. Press mixture firmly into prepared pan, smooth top with wet spatula. Top with remaining rice paper, press paper firmly onto mixture. Bake in moderately hot oven 25 minutes; cool in pan. Remove from pan before cutting with a serrated knife.

LEFT: Orange Hazelnut Crisps.
ABOVE: Spiced Choc Nut Panforte.

Left: Tray from House; china from Shop 60, The Old Ark Antique Market. Above: China from Waterford Wedgwood.

CRUNCHY CHOC PEANUT SLICE

4 x 60g Snickers bars, chopped
50g butter
1 tablespoon dark corn syrup
150g milk chocolate, chopped
½ cup (75g) unsalted roasted
**   peanuts, chopped**
2½ cups (175g) Crunchy Nut
**   Corn Flakes**

Grease 23cm square slab cake pan, place strip of baking paper to cover base and extend over 2 opposite sides.

Combine Snickers, butter, corn syrup and chocolate in large heatproof bowl, stir over pan of simmering water until smooth. Remove bowl from heat, stir in peanuts and Corn Flakes. Press mixture into prepared pan; refrigerate until set.

ALMOND HONEY SLICE

90g butter, melted
½ cup (100g) firmly packed
**   brown sugar**
1 cup (150g) plain flour
½ cup (60g) packaged
**   ground almonds**

TOPPING
125g butter, chopped
¼ cup (60ml) honey
1½ cups (210g) slivered almonds

Combine all ingredients in small bowl; mix well. Press mixture into 20cm x 30cm greased lamington pan. Bake in moderate oven about 12 minutes or until browned; cool. Spread with hot topping, bake in moderate oven about 15 minutes or until browned; cool in pan.

Topping: Combine butter and honey in small heavy-based pan, stir over heat until butter is melted. Simmer, uncovered, about 3 minutes or until mixture is a light caramel colour; stir in nuts.

BELOW: Crunchy Choc Peanut Slice.
RIGHT: Almond Honey Slice.

Right: Scales from House; board and ladle from Mosman Antiques.

CHRISTMAS CHESTNUT SLICE

Melted carob can be substituted for dark chocolate, if preferred.

½ x 700g packet fruit cake
250g packet cream cheese, softened
1 tablespoon dark rum
¾ cup (180ml) sweetened
  chestnut puree
250g packet Butternut Cookies,
  crushed
1½ cups (150g) walnuts,
  toasted, chopped
125g dark chocolate, melted

Cut cake into 5mm slices, place slices tightly in a single layer over base of greased 20cm x 30cm lamington pan. Beat cheese in medium bowl with electric mixer until smooth. Stir in rum, chestnut puree, cookie crumbs and nuts; mix well. Spread mixture over cake in pan; refrigerate until set. Drizzle with chocolate.

COFFEE ALMOND SHELLS

1 tablespoon dry instant coffee
2 teaspoons water
185g butter, chopped
¾ cup (150g) firmly packed
  brown sugar
1 egg yolk
1½ cups (225g) self-raising flour
¾ cup (90g) packaged
  ground almonds
¾ cup (60g) flaked almonds

Combine coffee with water, stir until dissolved. Beat butter, sugar and yolk in small bowl with electric mixer until smooth. Stir in coffee mixture, flour and ground nuts. Spoon mixture into piping bag fitted with 1.5cm star tube, pipe 5cm shell shapes about 5cm apart on greased oven trays, decorate with flaked nuts. Bake in moderate oven about 12 minutes or until firm; cool on wire racks.

Makes about 40.

LEFT: Christmas Chestnut Slice.
ABOVE: Coffee Almond Shells.

Left: China from Home & Garden on the Mall.

CHERRY CHOCODAMIA DIAMONDS

¾ cup (180ml) sweetened
   condensed milk
15g Copha
1 teaspoon grated orange rind
250g White Melts, finely chopped
1½ cups (225g) macadamias,
   toasted, coarsely chopped
1 cup (210g) red glace cherries,
   halved
1¼ cups (125g) plain sweet
   biscuit crumbs

Combine milk, Copha and rind in medium heavy-based pan, bring to boil, remove from heat, stir in White Melts, stir until smooth. Stir in nuts, cherries and crumbs. Press mixture evenly over base of greased 20cm x 30cm lamington pan; refrigerate until set.

LEFT: Cherry Chocodamia Diamonds.
ABOVE: Choc Chip Peanut Cookies.

Left: Wooden box from Plumes Gift Agencies.

CHOC CHIP PEANUT COOKIES

Chopped carob can be substituted for Choc Bits, if preferred.

125g butter, chopped
2 teaspoons vanilla essence
1 cup (220g) firmly packed
   brown sugar
1 egg
½ cup (130g) crunchy peanut butter
1½ cups (225g) plain flour
¾ cup (105g) unsalted roasted
   peanuts, chopped
1 cup (190g) Choc Bits

Beat butter, essence, sugar, egg and peanut butter in small bowl with electric mixer until smooth. Stir in flour, peanuts and Choc Bits. Roll rounded tablespoons of mixture into balls, place on ungreased oven trays, flatten slightly with a floured fork. Bake in moderate oven about 15 minutes or until browned; cool on trays.

Makes about 40.

CHOC NUT BISCOTTI

Carob powder can be substituted for cocoa, if preferred.

1 cup (220g) caster sugar
2 eggs
1⅔ cups (250g) plain flour
1 teaspoon baking powder
1 cup (150g) shelled pistachios, toasted
½ cup (70g) slivered almonds
¼ cup (25g) cocoa

Whisk sugar and eggs in small bowl until combined. Stir in flour, baking powder and nuts. Mix to a soft dough. Divide dough into 2 portions. Knead 1 portion on lightly floured surface until smooth but still slightly sticky. Divide this portion into 4 pieces. Roll each piece into a 25cm log shape. Knead remaining portion with cocoa until smooth, divide into 2 pieces. Roll each piece of chocolate mixture into a 25cm log shape.

Place 1 chocolate log on greased and floured oven tray. Place a plain log on each side, press gently together to form a slightly flattened shape. Repeat with remaining logs, using another greased and floured oven tray. Bake in moderate oven about 35 minutes or until dry. Cool 10 minutes on tray. Cut logs diagonally into 5mm slices with a serrated knife. Place in single layer on ungreased oven trays. Bake further 30 minutes in slow oven or until slices are dry.

Makes about 50.

RIGHT: Choc Nut Biscotti.

Tassels from Home & Garden on the Mall.

CARAMEL SEED SLICE

1 cup (220g) caster sugar
90g butter, chopped
½ cup (125ml) sweetened
  condensed milk
⅓ cup (80ml) glucose syrup
2 tablespoons golden syrup
2 tablespoons water
½ cup (75g) sesame seeds, toasted
½ cup (80g) sunflower seed kernels
¼ cup (35g) pepitas
½ cup (60g) chopped pecans
⅓ cup (50g) chopped dried apricots
3 cups (105g) Rice Bubbles
25 pecans, extra

Grease 26cm x 32cm Swiss roll pan; place strip of baking paper to cover base and extend over 2 opposite sides.

Combine sugar, butter, milk, glucose syrup, golden syrup and water in medium heavy-based pan, stir over heat, without boiling, until sugar is dissolved. Boil, stirring constantly, about 5 minutes or until mixture turns a caramel colour.

Stir in all seeds, chopped nuts, apricots and Rice Bubbles; quickly spread mixture evenly into prepared pan, top with extra pecans. Stand until just warm, mark into 25 squares. When completely cold, cut into squares.

Makes 25.

HAZELNUT CRESCENTS

125g butter, chopped
1 teaspoon vanilla essence
¼ cup (55g) caster sugar
¼ cup (50g) firmly packed
  brown sugar
1 egg
2 tablespoons cream
½ cup (55g) packaged ground
  hazelnuts
½ cup (75g) self-raising flour
1¼ cups (185g) plain flour
½ teaspoon ground cinnamon
½ cup (80g) icing sugar mixture,
  approximately

Beat butter, essence, caster sugar, brown sugar and egg in small bowl with electric mixer until smooth. Stir in cream, nuts, flours and cinnamon. Turn dough onto lightly floured surface, knead gently until smooth. Cover; refrigerate 30 minutes.

Shape level tablespoons of dough into crescents, place about 3cm apart on greased oven trays. Bake in moderate oven about 15 minutes or until browned. Lift crescents onto wire racks, sprinkle thickly with sifted icing sugar; cool.

Makes about 25.

LEFT: Caramel Seed Slice.
ABOVE: Hazelnut Crescents.

Above: Serviette and canister from Corso De' Fiori.

15

ALMOND JAM COOKIES

185g butter, chopped
1 teaspoon vanilla essence
¾ cup (165g) caster sugar
2 egg yolks
½ cup (60g) packaged
** ground almonds**
1½ cups (225g) plain flour
½ teaspoon baking powder
2 tablespoons apricot jam,
** approximately**
1 teaspoon grated lemon rind
2 tablespoons raspberry jam,
** approximately**

Beat butter, essence, sugar and yolks in medium bowl with electric mixer until just combined. Stir in nuts, flour and baking powder; mix well. Roll level tablespoons of mixture into balls, place about 5cm apart on ungreased oven trays. Press a hollow in each ball about 1cm deep and 1.5cm wide with the handle end of a lightly floured wooden spoon.

Combine apricot jam with half the rind. Combine raspberry jam with remaining rind. Carefully spoon a little apricot jam into half the cookies; spoon raspberry jam into remaining cookies. Bake in moderately slow oven about 25 minutes or until cookies are browned; cool on trays.

Makes about 30.

CHOC NUT CLUSTERS

Melted carob can be substituted for
Milk Melts, if preferred.

1½ cups (210g) slivered
** almonds, toasted**
½ cup (75g) chopped dried apricots
½ cup (95g) mixed dried fruit,
** chopped**
1⅓ cups (200g) Milk Melts, melted

Grease oven trays; cover trays with foil. Combine all ingredients in medium heatproof bowl; mix well. Place bowl over pan of hot water to prevent Milk Melts from setting too fast. Drop tablespoons of mixture onto prepared trays; refrigerate until firm.

Makes about 30.

LEFT: Almond Jam Cookies.
ABOVE: Choc Nut Clusters.

ORANGE PECAN DATE SLICE

100g butter, chopped
1 teaspoon vanilla essence
¼ cup (50g) firmly packed
    brown sugar
1 egg yolk
1 cup (150g) plain flour
½ teaspoon bicarbonate of soda
2 tablespoons pepitas, toasted
¼ cup (30g) finely chopped
    pecans, toasted

FILLING
1½ cups (240g) chopped
    seedless dates
1 teaspoon grated lemon rind
½ cup (125ml) orange juice
2 tablespoons caster sugar

TOPPING
5 egg whites
1¾ cups (215g) packaged
    ground almonds
⅔ cup (150g) caster sugar
2 teaspoons grated orange rind

Beat butter, essence, sugar and yolk in small bowl with electric mixer until smooth. Stir in flour, soda, pepitas and nuts, spread evenly over base of greased 20cm x 30cm lamington pan. Bake in moderate oven about 15 minutes or until browned; cool. Spread filling over base, spread with topping. Bake in moderately hot oven about 20 minutes or until browned; cool in pan.

Filling: Combine all ingredients in small pan, stir over heat about 5 minutes or until mixture is thick; cool 10 minutes.

Topping: Combine all ingredients in bowl; mix well.

ALMOND SESAME CRISPS

90g butter, chopped
½ cup (110g) caster sugar
1 egg
1 tablespoon tahini
¼ teaspoon orange flower water
¼ teaspoon ground cardamom
¾ cup (110g) plain flour
½ cup (60g) packaged
    ground almonds
¼ cup (35g) shelled pistachios,
    chopped, toasted
2 tablespoons sesame seeds

Beat butter, sugar, egg, tahini, orange flower water and cardamom in small bowl with electric mixer until smooth. Stir in flour and nuts, mix to a soft dough. Shape into a 24cm log, roll in seeds. Wrap log in plastic; refrigerate until firm.

Cut log into 5mm slices, place slices about 6cm apart on greased oven trays. Bake in moderately hot oven about 7 minutes or until browned. Stand 2 minutes before lifting onto wire racks to cool.

Makes about 35.

ABOVE: Orange Pecan Date Slice.
RIGHT: Almond Sesame Crisps.

Right: Setting from Barbara's Storehouse.

POPPYSEED HONEY PINWHEELS

125g butter, chopped
½ teaspoon vanilla essence
½ cup (110g) caster sugar
1 egg
1⅔ cups (250g) plain flour

FILLING
⅓ cup (50g) finely chopped
   macadamias
½ cup (80g) poppyseeds
¼ cup (60ml) warmed honey
1 teaspoon grated orange rind

Beat butter, essence, sugar and egg in small bowl with electric mixer until smooth. Stir in flour; press dough into a ball, wrap in plastic wrap; refrigerate 30 minutes.

Divide dough into 2 portions. Roll each portion between sheets of baking paper to a 20cm x 25cm rectangle, spread with filling. Roll rectangles from short side like a Swiss roll, cover; refrigerate until firm. Cut rolls into 5mm slices, place about 2cm apart on ungreased oven trays. Bake in moderately hot oven about 10 minutes or until browned; cool on trays.

Filling: Combine all ingredients in bowl; mix well.

Makes about 40.

HAZELNUT CHOC FLECK COOKIES

Chopped carob can be substituted for dark chocolate, if preferred.

185g butter, chopped
½ cup (110g) caster sugar
1 egg
1 cup (150g) plain flour
1¼ cups (135g) packaged
   ground hazelnuts
100g dark chocolate, finely chopped

Grease 2 oven trays, cover trays with baking paper.

Beat butter, sugar and egg in small bowl with electric mixer until smooth. Stir in remaining ingredients; mix well. Drop slightly rounded tablespoons of mixture about 5cm apart onto prepared trays. Bake in moderate oven about 15 minutes or until browned. Stand 5 minutes before lifting onto wire racks to cool.

Makes about 20.

ABOVE: Hazelnut Choc Fleck Cookies.
RIGHT: Poppyseed Honey Pinwheels.

Above: China from Accoutrement; basket from Barbara's Storehouse. Right: Setting from Barbara's Storehouse.

PISTACHIO CHOCOLATE BISCUITS

Melted carob can be substituted for dark chocolate, if preferred.

½ cup (75g) shelled pistachios
1 cup (150g) plain flour
¼ cup (35g) self-raising flour
¾ cup (120g) icing sugar mixture
60g butter, chopped
1 egg
2 teaspoons water
80g dark chocolate, melted
⅓ cup (50g) shelled chopped
    pistachios, extra

Process the ½ cup of nuts until finely ground. Add flours, sugar and butter, process until mixture resembles fine crumbs. Add egg and water, process until ingredients cling together. Wrap in plastic wrap; refrigerate 30 minutes.

Divide dough into 2 portions, roll each portion between sheets of baking paper until 5mm thick. Cut into 5cm rounds, place rounds on greased oven trays.

Bake in moderate oven about 10 minutes or until browned; cool on trays. Spread cold biscuits with chocolate, sprinkle with extra nuts.

Makes about 40.

GLACE PEACH AND PEPITA SLICE

90g butter, melted
1 teaspoon grated lime rind
2 eggs, lightly beaten
¾ cup (150g) firmly packed
    brown sugar
½ cup (75g) self-raising flour
½ cup (75g) cornflour
½ cup (75g) pepitas
½ cup (75g) macadamias, toasted,
    chopped
½ cup (50g) walnuts, toasted,
    chopped
⅓ cup (85g) chopped glace peaches
¼ cup (30g) oat bran
2 teaspoons ground ginger

Grease 20cm x 30cm lamington pan, place a strip of greased foil to cover base and extend over 2 opposite sides.

Combine all ingredients in large bowl; mix well. Spread mixture into prepared pan. Bake in moderately hot oven about 20 minutes or until lightly browned. Stand slice 5 minutes before turning onto wire rack, remove foil; cool.

LEFT: Pistachio Chocolate Biscuits.
BELOW: Glace Peach and Pepita Slice.

ALMOND CRISPS

125g butter, chopped
¼ cup (55g) caster sugar
1 cup (150g) self-raising flour
¼ cup (30g) packaged
   ground almonds
2 tablespoons flaked almonds

Beat butter and sugar in small bowl with electric mixer until smooth. Stir in flour and ground nuts. Roll level tablespoons of mixture into balls, place about 5cm apart on greased oven trays. Flatten slightly with a floured fork to 1cm thick, sprinkle with flaked nuts. Bake in moderately hot oven about 10 minutes or until browned. Stand 5 minutes before lifting onto wire racks to cool.

Makes about 15.

LEMON POPPYSEED SHORTBREAD BARS

200g butter, chopped
2 teaspoons grated lemon rind
½ cup (80g) icing sugar mixture
2 cups (300g) plain flour
1½ tablespoons poppyseeds
1 tablespoon lemon juice

Beat butter, rind and sugar in medium bowl with electric mixer until light and fluffy. Stir in flour, seeds and juice. Press mixture together firmly. Press into greased 20cm x 30cm lamington pan, mark into finger lengths. Bake in moderately slow oven about 35 minutes or until browned. Cut into finger lengths in pan; cool in pan. Serve dusted with a little extra sifted icing sugar, if desired.

BELOW: Almond Crisps.
RIGHT: Lemon Poppyseed Shortbread Bars.

ALMOND MAPLE GEMS

These cookies do not contain flour.

**2 cups (250g) packaged
   ground almonds**
**½ cup (80g) finely chopped
   seedless dates**
⅓ cup (75g) caster sugar
1 teaspoon grated orange rind
¼ cup (60ml) maple-flavoured syrup
1 egg white, lightly beaten
1 cup (50g) flaked coconut, crushed

Combine nuts, dates, sugar and rind in medium bowl, stir in maple syrup and egg white; mix well. Roll rounded teaspoons of mixture into balls, toss in coconut, press coconut on firmly. Place balls about 3cm apart on greased oven trays. Bake in moderate oven about 10 minutes or until browned; cool on trays.

Makes about 40.

CHOCOLATE HAZELNUT SLICE

1 cup (150g) self-raising flour
½ cup (45g) coconut
**½ cup (55g) packaged
   ground hazelnuts**
**1 cup (200g) firmly packed
   brown sugar**
125g butter, melted
⅔ cup (160ml) Milky Way Spread

Combine flour, coconut, nuts, sugar and butter in medium bowl; mix well. Press into greased 20cm x 30cm lamington pan. Bake in moderate oven about 15 minutes or until firm; cool 5 minutes. Spread Milky Way over base, bake in moderate oven about 10 minutes or until set; cool in pan. Cut with a hot knife; serve dusted with sifted icing sugar, if desired.

ABOVE: Almond Maple Gems.
RIGHT: Chocolate Hazelnut Slice.

*Above: Rosenthal plate by Versace exclusively for
David Jones. Right: China from Waterford Wedgwood.*

CARAMEL NUT CRUNCH

Chopped carob can be substituted for dark chocolate, if preferred.

250g dark chocolate, finely chopped
20g butter
250g packet Scotch Finger biscuits

TOPPING
300ml cream
1 teaspoon vanilla essence
20g butter
½ cup (125ml) honey
1 cup (200g) firmly packed
   brown sugar
½ cup (75g) macadamias, toasted,
   coarsely chopped
½ cup (80g) pine nuts, toasted
½ cup (50g) pecans, toasted,
   coarsely chopped
½ cup (75g) shelled pistachios,
   toasted, coarsely chopped

Line base and sides of 23cm square slab cake pan with plastic wrap. Melt chocolate and butter in small heatproof bowl over pan of simmering water, spread over base of prepared pan. Halve biscuits lengthways, place over chocolate, press lightly; set at room temperature. Spread topping over base; refrigerate until set.

Topping: Combine cream, essence, butter, honey and sugar in medium heavy-based pan, stir over low heat, without boiling, until sugar is dissolved. Boil rapidly about 20 minutes, without stirring, until mixture turns a caramel colour and reaches 122˚C on a candy thermometer. Stir in nuts.

ABOVE: Caramel Nut Crunch.
RIGHT: Hazelnut, Fig and Ricotta Slice.

Right: Setting from Opus.

HAZELNUT, FIG AND RICOTTA SLICE

Milk or brandy can be substituted for Frangelico, if preferred.

100g butter, chopped
⅓ cup (65g) firmly packed
   brown sugar
1 egg
1 cup (150g) self-raising flour
½ cup (75g) plain flour
½ cup (55g) packaged
   ground hazelnuts

FILLING
400g ricotta cheese
½ cup (110g) caster sugar
½ cup (60g) chopped
   roasted hazelnuts
2 tablespoons Frangelico
¼ cup (45g) chopped dried figs

Process all ingredients until crumbly; do not over-process. Press half the mixture over base of greased 20cm x 30cm lamington pan. Pour filling over base; sprinkle with remaining base mixture. Bake in moderate oven about 45 minutes or until slice is firm.

Filling: Combine all ingredients in medium bowl; mix well.

FLORENTINE JEWELS

Melted carob can be substituted for Choc Melts, if preferred.

1 cup (150g) Choc Melts, melted
¼ cup (55g) caster sugar
1 tablespoon water
2 teaspoons coarsely grated lemon rind
1 tablespoon glucose syrup
2 tablespoons sweetened
**   condensed milk**
¼ cup (20g) flaked almonds, toasted
¼ cup (35g) shelled pistachios,
**   toasted, chopped**
1 tablespoon finely chopped mixed peel
1 tablespoon finely chopped red
**   glace cherries**

Cover oven tray with baking paper, mark 16 x 5cm rounds on paper. Spread Choc Melts to cover each round about 4mm thick; refrigerate until set.

Combine sugar, water, rind and glucose syrup in small heavy-based pan, stir over heat, without boiling, until sugar is dissolved. Add milk, boil about 2 minutes, stirring, until mixture just changes colour. Remove from heat, stir in nuts, peel and cherries. Drop rounded teaspoons of mixture onto chocolate rounds; refrigerate until set.

Makes 16.

HAZELNUT FUDGE TRIANGLES

250g packet Granita biscuits
½ cup (55g) packaged
**   ground hazelnuts**
100g butter, melted
1 tablespoon golden syrup

FILLING
125g butter, chopped
½ cup (110g) caster sugar
4 egg yolks
½ cup (125ml) Nutella
1 tablespoon Creme de Cacao
1 cup (150g) roasted hazelnuts,
**   chopped**

Grease 20cm x 30cm lamington pan, place strip of foil to cover base and extend over 2 opposite sides.

Process biscuits and nuts until finely ground. Add butter and golden syrup, process until combined. Press mixture into prepared pan; refrigerate 30 minutes. Bake base in moderate oven about 10 minutes or until firm; cool. Spread filling over base, bake 20 minutes or until firm. Cool in pan; refrigerate until firm. Serve dusted with sifted icing sugar, if desired.
Filling: Beat butter and sugar in small bowl with electric mixer until smooth. Add yolks 1 at a time, beating well after each addition. Add Nutella and liqueur, beat until just combined. Stir in nuts.

LEFT: Hazelnut Fudge Triangles.
RIGHT: Florentine Jewels.

Left: Setting from House.

CITRUS SUNFLOWER BISCUITS

125g butter, chopped
2 teaspoons grated lemon rind
2 teaspoons grated orange rind
¾ cup (165g) caster sugar
1 egg
1½ cups (225g) plain flour
½ cup (45g) coconut
¼ cup (40g) sunflower seed kernels
silver cachous

Beat butter, rinds, sugar and egg in small bowl with electric mixer until smooth. Stir in flour, coconut and kernels. Drop level tablespoons of mixture about 3cm apart on greased oven trays, flatten slightly with a floured fork; top with cachous. Bake in moderate oven about 20 minutes or until browned. Cool on trays.

Makes about 30.

COCONUT APRICOT SLICE

1 cup (150g) self-raising flour
½ teaspoon ground cinnamon
¾ cup (65g) coconut
¾ cup (150g) firmly packed brown sugar
⅓ cup (50g) chopped dried apricots
⅓ cup (40g) chopped pecans
100g butter, melted
2 eggs, lightly beaten
½ cup (125ml) buttermilk

CREAM CHEESE FROSTING
90g packaged cream cheese, chopped
60g butter
1 tablespoon golden syrup
⅔ cup (110g) icing sugar mixture

Combine all ingredients in medium bowl; mix well. Pour mixture into greased 26cm x 32cm Swiss roll pan. Bake in moderate oven about 25 minutes or until firm; cool in pan. Spread slice with cream cheese frosting; refrigerate before cutting.

Cream Cheese Frosting: Beat cheese, butter and golden syrup in small bowl with electric mixer until smooth. Gradually beat in icing sugar.

ABOVE: Coconut Apricot Slice.
RIGHT: Citrus Sunflower Biscuits.

LIME COCONUT SHORTBREAD

185g butter, chopped
1 teaspoon coconut essence
2 teaspoons grated lime rind
⅓ cup (75g) caster sugar
1½ cups (225g) plain flour
¼ cup (35g) rice flour
⅓ cup (30g) coconut

Beat butter, essence, rind and sugar in medium bowl with electric mixer until smooth. Stir in flours and coconut in 2 batches. Knead dough gently on lightly floured surface until smooth. Roll dough between sheets of baking paper until 4mm thick, cut into 6cm shapes, place about 3cm apart on greased oven trays. Bake in moderate oven about 10 minutes or until firm. Stand shortbread 3 minutes before lifting onto wire racks to cool.

Makes about 45.

MARMALADE ALMOND COCONUT SQUARES

125g butter, chopped
1 teaspoon almond essence
¼ cup (55g) caster sugar
1 cup (150g) plain flour
¼ cup (20g) coconut
⅓ cup (15g) flaked coconut
¼ cup (60ml) marmalade, warmed

TOPPING
90g butter, chopped
2 teaspoons grated orange rind
⅓ cup (75g) caster sugar
2 eggs
1 cup (90g) coconut
1 cup (125g) packaged ground almonds

Beat butter, essence and sugar in small bowl with electric mixer until smooth. Stir in flour and coconut, press into greased 19cm x 29cm rectangular slice pan. Bake in moderately hot oven about 15 minutes or until browned. Spread hot slice with topping; sprinkle with flaked coconut. Bake in moderate oven about 20 minutes or until firm. Brush hot slice with marmalade; cool in pan.

Topping: Beat butter, rind and sugar in small bowl with electric mixer until smooth, add eggs, beat until combined (mixture will look curdled at this stage). Stir in coconut and nuts.

LEFT: Lime Coconut Shortbread.
RIGHT: Marmalade Almond Coconut Squares.

Left and right: China from Waterford Wedgwood.

HONEY MACADAMIA COOKIES

125g butter, melted
2 tablespoons honey
¼ cup (55g) caster sugar
1 teaspoon bicarbonate of soda
¾ cup (50g) shredded coconut
1¼ cups (185g) plain flour
¼ cup (35g) macadamias,
**   finely chopped**
2 tablespoons demerara sugar,
**   approximately**

Beat butter, honey, caster sugar and soda in small bowl with electric mixer until smooth. Stir in coconut, flour and nuts. Roll rounded teaspoons of mixture into balls, press 1 side of each ball into demerara sugar, place about 4cm apart on greased oven trays; flatten slightly. Bake in moderate oven about 10 minutes or until browned. Stand cookies 5 minutes before lifting onto wire racks to cool.

Makes about 35.

COCONUT ALMOND BISCOTTI

1 cup (220g) caster sugar
2 eggs
1 teaspoon grated orange rind
1⅓ cups (200g) plain flour
⅓ cup (50g) self-raising flour
⅔ cup (45g) shredded coconut
1 cup (160g) blanched almonds

Whisk sugar, eggs and rind together in medium bowl. Stir in flours, coconut and nuts; mix to a sticky dough. Divide dough into 2 portions. Using floured hands, roll each portion into a 20cm log, place on greased oven tray. Bake in moderate oven about 35 minutes or until lightly browned; cool on tray.

Cut logs diagonally into 1cm slices, using a serrated knife. Place slices, cut side up, on oven trays. Bake in moderately slow oven about 25 minutes or until dry and crisp, turning over halfway through cooking; cool on trays.

Makes about 30.

LEFT: Honey Macadamia Cookies.
ABOVE: Coconut Almond Biscotti.

Left: Setting from Opus. Above: Plate from The Bay Tree Kitchen Shop.

RICH COCONUT CREAM SLICE

½ cup (75g) plain flour
½ cup (75g) self-raising flour
¾ cup (65g) coconut
⅓ cup (65g) firmly packed
 brown sugar
125g butter, melted
½ cup (80g) blanched almonds,
 approximately

TOPPING
400g can sweetened condensed milk
2 tablespoons golden syrup
2 tablespoons brown sugar
½ cup (45g) coconut
½ cup (125ml) coconut cream

Grease 20cm x 30cm lamington pan, place strip of baking paper to cover base and extend over 2 opposite sides.

Combine flours, coconut, sugar and butter in medium bowl; mix well; press over base of prepared pan. Bake in moderate oven about 20 minutes or until firm.

Spread hot topping over hot base, top with nuts about 2cm apart. Bake in moderate oven about 20 minutes or until browned; cool in pan. Refrigerate until firm.

Topping: Combine milk, golden syrup and sugar in medium heavy-based pan, stir over heat until mixture boils, simmer, stirring, about 5 minutes or until light honey colour. Stir in coconut and cream.

COCONUT TUILES

1 egg white
¼ cup (55g) caster sugar
2 tablespoons plain flour
30g butter, melted
¼ teaspoon coconut essence
2 tablespoons shredded coconut

Beat egg white in small bowl with electric mixer until soft peaks form, gradually add sugar, beating until dissolved between additions. Fold in flour, butter and essence.

Drop 2 level teaspoons of mixture together onto greased oven trays; allow 4 tuiles per tray. Spread mixture into 7cm rounds, sprinkle with coconut. Bake in moderate oven about 5 minutes or until lightly browned.

Slide a metal spatula under each tuile, then quickly shape over a rolling pin; leave until firm.

Makes about 15.

BELOW: Rich Coconut Cream Slice.
RIGHT: Coconut Tuiles.

Below: Setting from Opus. Right: Setting from Art House.

FUDGY CHOC CHERRY COOKIES

1⅓ cups (200g) Milk Melts
60g butter
¼ cup (60ml) vegetable oil
⅓ cup (75g) caster sugar
2 eggs, lightly beaten
1 cup (150g) self-raising flour
1 cup (150g) plain flour
3 x 85g Cherry Ripe bars, chopped
¾ cup (110g) Milk Melts, melted, extra
1 tablespoon vegetable oil, extra

Combine Milk Melts, butter, oil and sugar in medium pan, stir over low heat until Milk Melts have melted; cool to room temperature. Stir in eggs, flours and two-thirds of the Cherry Ripe bars. Roll level tablespoons of mixture into balls, place about 3cm apart on greased oven trays. Bake in moderate oven about 15 minutes or until lightly browned. Cool on trays.

Spread tops of cookies with combined extra Milk Melts and extra oil, sprinkle with remaining Cherry Ripe bars.

Makes about 35.

CHOC GINGER RAISIN SLICE

If preferred, ¼ cup (25g) carob powder can be substituted for the drinking chocolate and cocoa. Chopped carob can be substituted for the dark chocolate.

125g butter, chopped
¼ cup (55g) caster sugar
2 tablespoons golden syrup
2 tablespoons drinking chocolate
1 tablespoon cocoa
2 tablespoons milk
250g packet plain sweet biscuits, crushed
2 cups (200g) plain cake crumbs
¼ cup (50g) chopped glace ginger
⅓ cup (55g) chopped raisins

TOPPING
125g dark chocolate, melted
10g butter, melted

Grease 20cm x 30cm lamington pan, place strip of baking paper to cover base and extend over 2 opposite sides.

Combine butter, sugar and golden syrup in medium heavy-based pan, stir over heat, without boiling, until sugar is dissolved. Stir in remaining ingredients; mix well. Spread mixture into prepared pan, spread with topping; refrigerate slice until set.

Topping: Combine chocolate and butter in small bowl, stir until smooth.

ABOVE: Fudgy Choc Cherry Cookies.
RIGHT: Choc Ginger Raisin Slice.

Right: Box from David Jones.

CHOC CHERRY CRACKLES

Carob powder can be substituted for cocoa, if preferred.

250g Copha, chopped
1 cup (160g) icing sugar mixture
1/3 cup (35g) cocoa
4 cups (140g) Rice Bubbles
2/3 cup (60g) coconut
1/2 cup (105g) glace cherries, finely chopped

Place Copha in large pan, stir over heat until melted; cool to room temperature; do not allow to set. Stir in remaining ingredients; mix well. Drop rounded tablespoons of mixture into paper patty cases; refrigerate until firm.

Makes about 30.

CHOCOLATE RAINBOW SLICE

250g packet Golliwog biscuits, crushed
125g butter, melted
400g can sweetened condensed milk
1/2 cup (45g) coconut
1 cup (150g) unsalted roasted peanuts, chopped
250g packet Smarties

Grease 20cm x 30cm lamington pan, place strip of greased foil to cover base and extend over 2 opposite sides.

Combine biscuit crumbs and butter in small bowl; press over base of prepared pan; refrigerate 30 minutes.

Combine remaining ingredients in medium bowl, mix well; spread over base. Bake in moderate oven about 30 minutes or until lightly browned; cool in pan. Refrigerate slice before cutting.

LEFT: Choc Cherry Crackles.
ABOVE: Chocolate Rainbow Slice.

43

DOUBLE CHOCOLATE CHIP COOKIES

Carob, chopped to required size, can be substituted for Choc Bits and Milk Melts, if preferred.

250g butter, chopped
1 teaspoon vanilla essence
⅔ cup (130g) firmly packed
 brown sugar
⅔ cup (150g) caster sugar
2 eggs, lightly beaten
2½ cups (375g) plain flour
1 teaspoon bicarbonate of soda
½ cup (60g) chopped walnuts,
 toasted
1 cup (190g) Choc Bits
1 cup (150g) Milk Melts, halved
⅓ cup (65g) Choc Bits, extra
½ cup (75g) Milk Melts,
 quartered, extra

Beat butter, essence, sugars and eggs in medium bowl with electric mixer until smooth. Stir in dry ingredients, nuts, Choc Bits and Milk Melts; mix well.

Drop level tablespoons of mixture about 5cm apart onto greased oven trays. Press extra Choc Bits and extra Milk Melts into cookies. Bake in moderately hot oven about 12 minutes or until lightly browned. Stand cookies 2 minutes before lifting onto wire racks to cool.

Makes about 50.

PEANUT BUTTER CHOCOLATE SLICE

Melted carob can be substituted for dark chocolate, if preferred.

3 eggs, lightly beaten
1 teaspoon vanilla essence
1 cup (200g) firmly packed
 brown sugar
¾ cup (110g) plain flour
¼ cup (35g) self-raising flour
125g butter, melted
250g dark chocolate, melted
¾ cup (195g) crunchy peanut butter
1 cup (150g) unsalted roasted
 peanuts, chopped

Grease 20cm x 30cm lamington pan, place strip of foil to cover base and extend over 2 opposite sides.

Beat eggs, essence and sugar in medium bowl with electric mixer about 3 minutes or until thick and pale in colour. Stir in remaining ingredients. Spread mixture into prepared pan. Bake in moderately slow oven 30 minutes or until firm; cool in pan.

LEFT: Double Chocolate Chip Cookies.
RIGHT: Peanut Butter Chocolate Slice.

Left: Tray and plate from Statements. Right: Cupboard and box from Mosman Antiques – Rustic Rumours.

DOUBLE CHOC ALMOND SLICE

250g White Melts, melted
2 tablespoons vegetable oil
1 cup (160g) almond kernels, toasted
250g dark chocolate, finely chopped
⅔ cup (160ml) sweetened
**   condensed milk**
30g butter
¼ teaspoon orange essence

Spread combined White Melts and oil over base of oiled 19cm x 29cm rectangular slice pan, sprinkle with nuts; refrigerate until set.

Combine dark chocolate, condensed milk and butter in medium heavy-based pan, stir constantly over low heat until smooth, add essence. Spread mixture quickly over base; refrigerate until set.

SUPER RICH CHOCOLATE TEMPTATIONS

Carob powder can be substituted for cocoa, and chopped carob for Choc Bits and Choc Melts, if preferred. For a chewy biscuit, bake about 12 minutes. If you like a crunchier biscuit, bake about further 5 minutes.

125g butter, chopped
1 teaspoon vanilla essence
1¼ cups (250g) firmly packed
**   brown sugar**
1 egg
1 cup (150g) plain flour
¼ cup (35g) self-raising flour
1 teaspoon bicarbonate of soda
⅓ cup (35g) cocoa
¾ cup (90g) chopped pecans, toasted
½ cup (85g) chopped raisins
½ cup (95g) Choc Bits
½ cup (75g) Choc Melts, halved

Beat butter, essence, sugar and egg in medium bowl with electric mixer until smooth. Stir in remaining ingredients; mix well. Drop slightly rounded tablespoons of mixture about 5cm apart onto greased oven trays. Bake in moderate oven about 12 minutes or until firm; cool on trays.

Makes about 24.

LEFT: Double Choc Almond Slice.
BELOW: Super Rich Chocolate Temptations.

Below: Fabric from Adorabella.

47

ROCKY CHOCS

Carob powder can be substituted for cocoa, and chopped carob for Choc Bits, if preferred.

200g butter, chopped
¾ cup (165g) caster sugar
¾ cup (150g) firmly packed brown sugar
2 eggs
2 cups (300g) self-raising flour
½ cup (50g) cocoa
½ cup (125g) chopped glace cherries
½ cup (95g) Choc Bits
½ cup (75g) unsalted roasted peanuts

Beat butter, sugars and eggs in medium bowl with electric mixer until smooth. Stir in remaining ingredients; mix well. Roll level tablespoons of mixture into balls, place about 3cm apart on greased oven trays. Bake in moderate oven about 15 minutes or until firm. Stand biscuits 5 minutes before lifting onto wire racks to cool.

Makes about 45.

WHITE CHOCODAMIA COOKIES

125g butter, chopped
1 teaspoon vanilla essence
1 teaspoon grated orange rind
1 cup (200g) firmly packed brown sugar
1 egg
1½ cups (225g) plain flour
1 cup (190g) White Bits
⅓ cup (50g) finely chopped macadamias

Beat butter, essence, rind, sugar and egg in small bowl with electric mixer until smooth. Stir in flour and White Bits. Drop level tablespoons of mixture about 5cm apart onto greased oven trays, top with nuts. Bake cookies in moderate oven about 15 minutes or until firm. Cool on wire racks.

Makes about 30.

ABOVE: Rocky Chocs.
RIGHT: White Chocodamia Cookies.

TRIPLE CHOCOLATE SLICE

125g butter, chopped
90g dark chocolate, chopped
90g milk chocolate, chopped
½ cup (100g) firmly packed brown sugar
2 eggs, lightly beaten
1 cup (150g) plain flour
⅔ cup (130g) White Bits

Grease deep 19cm square cake pan, place strip of baking paper to cover base and extend over 2 opposite sides.

Combine butter with dark and milk chocolate in medium pan, stir over heat until chocolate is melted; cool 2 minutes. Stir in remaining ingredients; mix well. Pour mixture into prepared pan. Bake in moderate oven about 30 minutes; cool in pan. Serve slice dusted with sifted icing sugar, if desired.

CHOCOLATE CORNFLAKE CRUNCH

80g butter, chopped
2 tablespoons golden syrup
½ cup (75g) Choc Melts
½ cup (75g) White Melts
½ cup (40g) flaked almonds, toasted
2½ cups (75g) Corn Flakes
½ cup (35g) shredded coconut, toasted

Combine butter, golden syrup and both Melts in medium heavy-based pan, stir over low heat until chocolate is melted. Gently stir in remaining ingredients. Press mixture into greased 20cm round sandwich cake pan; refrigerate until firm.

ABOVE: Triple Chocolate Slice.
RIGHT: Chocolate Cornflake Crunch.

Above: China from Accoutrement; fabric from Adorabella.

CAROB HONEY BARS

Choc Melts or chopped chocolate can be substituted for carob buttons, if preferred.

60g butter
1⅓ cups (200g) carob buttons
¼ cup (60ml) honey
½ cup (125ml) sweetened condensed milk
250g packet Granita biscuits, crushed
¼ cup (40g) blanched almonds, toasted

Combine butter, carob, honey and condensed milk in medium heavy-based pan, stir over heat until butter and carob are just melted, stir in biscuit crumbs. Press mixture into greased deep 19cm square cake pan, press nuts onto slice. Refrigerate slice until firm.

MOCHA MACADAMIA COOKIES

125g butter, chopped
1 teaspoon vanilla essence
1¼ cups (250g) firmly packed brown sugar
1 egg
3 teaspoons dry instant coffee
1 tablespoon Tia Maria or Kahlua
2 tablespoons cocoa
1½ cups (225g) plain flour
1¼ cups (185g) chopped macadamias, toasted
⅓ cup (70g) chocolate-coated coffee beans, approximately

Beat butter, essence, sugar and egg with combined coffee and liqueur in medium bowl with electric mixer until smooth. Stir in dry ingredients and nuts. Drop level tablespoons of mixture about 5cm apart onto greased oven trays, flatten slightly with a floured fork, top with coffee beans. Bake in moderate oven about 15 minutes or until firm.

Makes about 35.

LEFT: Carob Honey Bars.
ABOVE: Mocha Macadamia Cookies.

Above: Placemat and bookends from Opus.

DECADENT CHOCOLATE LIQUEUR SLICE

Melted carob can be substituted for dark chocolate, if preferred.

125g dark chocolate, melted
4 egg whites
¾ cup (165g) caster sugar
1 cup (110g) packaged ground hazelnuts
2 tablespoons plain flour

TOPPING
125g butter, chopped
½ cup (110g) caster sugar
4 egg yolks
1 tablespoon Grand Marnier
200g dark chocolate, melted

Line base and sides of 20cm x 30cm lamington pan with foil; spread with chocolate. Refrigerate 10 minutes or until set.

Beat egg whites in small bowl with electric mixer until soft peaks form, gradually add sugar, beating until dissolved between additions. Fold in nuts and flour; spread over chocolate base. Bake in moderate oven about 20 minutes or until firm; cool 20 minutes. Spread slice with topping, bake further 15 minutes; cool in pan. Refrigerate until firm.

Topping: Beat butter, sugar, yolks and liqueur in small bowl with electric mixer until sugar is dissolved; stir in chocolate.

CHOC MINT ALMOND BISCUITS

Carob powder can be substituted for cocoa, and melted carob for Choc Melts, if preferred.

1¼ cups (185g) plain flour
1 cup (160g) icing sugar mixture
2 tablespoons cocoa
1 cup (125g) packaged ground almonds
125g butter, chopped
1 teaspoon peppermint essence
1 egg
1 cup (150g) Choc Melts, melted
1 tablespoon vegetable oil
1 teaspoon peppermint essence, extra

Process flour, sugar, cocoa, nuts and butter until mixture resembles breadcrumbs. Add essence and egg, process until mixture forms a ball. Knead dough gently on floured surface until smooth, cover; refrigerate 30 minutes.

Roll dough between sheets of baking paper until 4mm thick. Cut dough into 5cm squares, place about 3cm apart on greased oven trays. Bake in moderate oven about 12 minutes or until firm. Cool on trays. Dip half of each biscuit in combined Choc Melts, oil and extra essence. Place biscuits on foil-covered trays; stand at room temperature until set.

Makes about 35.

LEFT: Decadent Chocolate Liqueur Slice.
BELOW: Choc Mint Almond Biscuits.

CHEWY CHOCOLATE MUESLI BROWNIES

Chopped carob can be substituted for dark chocolate, and carob powder for cocoa, if preferred.

125g butter, chopped
100g dark chocolate, chopped
1 cup (220g) caster sugar
2 eggs, lightly beaten
1 cup (150g) plain flour
¼ cup (25g) cocoa
½ cup (60g) chopped pecans
½ cup (65g) toasted muesli

Grease 23cm square slab cake pan, place strip of foil to cover base and extend over 2 opposite sides.

Combine butter, chocolate and sugar in medium heavy-based pan, stir over low heat until chocolate is melted; cool 2 minutes. Stir in remaining ingredients. Pour mixture into prepared pan. Bake in moderate oven about 30 minutes or until firm; cool in pan. Serve dusted with a little sifted drinking chocolate, if desired.

CHOCOLATE RUM AND RAISIN SLICE

Chopped carob can be substituted for dark chocolate, if preferred.

125g butter, chopped
200g dark chocolate, chopped
½ cup (110g) caster sugar
1 cup (170g) finely chopped raisins
2 eggs, lightly beaten
1½ cups (225g) plain flour
1 tablespoon dark rum

Combine butter, chocolate, sugar and raisins in medium heavy-based pan, stir over low heat until chocolate is melted; cool to room temperature. Stir in remaining ingredients; mix well. Spread mixture into greased 20cm x 30cm lamington pan. Bake in moderately slow oven about 30 minutes or until just firm; cool in pan. Serve slice dusted with sifted icing sugar, if desired.

ABOVE: Chewy Chocolate Muesli Brownies.
RIGHT: Chocolate Rum and Raisin Slice.

Above: China from Villeroy & Boch. Right: China and serviette from Opus.

HONEYCOMB CHOCOLATE ROUGHS

⅔ cup (100g) Milk Melts, melted
1 tablespoon cream
2 tablespoons golden syrup
¼ cup (40g) chopped sultanas
½ cup (75g) chopped macadamias, toasted
2 x 50g Violet Crumble bars, chopped

Combine all ingredients in medium bowl. Drop rounded teaspoons of mixture onto foil-covered trays; refrigerate until set.

Makes about 30.

MOCHA CREAM CHEESE SLICE

1½ packets (300g) Lattice biscuits
2 teaspoons gelatine
¼ cup (60ml) water
125g unsalted butter, chopped
375g packaged cream cheese, chopped
1 cup (220g) caster sugar
¼ cup (60ml) Nutella
1 tablespoon Kahlua or Tia Maria
2 teaspoons dry instant coffee

Cover base of 23cm square slab cake pan with half the biscuits. Sprinkle gelatine over water in cup, stand in small pan of simmering water, stir until dissolved. Beat butter, cheese and sugar in small bowl with electric mixer until light and fluffy. Beat in Nutella and combined liqueur and coffee. Spread mixture over biscuits, top with remaining biscuits; refrigerate until set.

ABOVE: Honeycomb Chocolate Roughs.
ABOVE RIGHT: Almond Nougat Cheesecake Slice.
RIGHT: Mocha Cream Cheese Slice.

Above right: China from Waterford Wedgwood.

ALMOND NOUGAT CHEESECAKE SLICE

200g Golliwog biscuits
½ cup (60g) packaged ground almonds
125g butter, melted

FILLING
500g packaged cream cheese,
chopped
½ cup (110g) caster sugar
2 eggs
2 x 100g Toblerone bars,
chopped, melted
½ cup (125ml) thickened cream
2 x 45g Almond Nougat bars,
finely chopped

Grease 20cm x 30cm lamington pan, place strip of foil to cover base and extend over 2 opposite sides.

Process biscuits and nuts until finely crushed. Add butter, process until combined. Press mixture into prepared pan, refrigerate 30 minutes.

Pour filling over base. Bake in moderately slow oven about 40 minutes or until just set; cool in pan. Refrigerate slice several hours or overnight.

Cut slice using hot knife, decorate with whipped cream and extra chopped Toblerone, if desired.

Filling: Beat cheese and sugar in medium bowl with electric mixer until smooth. Add eggs 1 at a time, beating well between additions. Add Toblerone and cream, beat until combined; stir in Almond Nougat bars.

MAPLE SYRUP TUILES

60g butter
⅓ cup (65g) firmly packed
**   brown sugar**
1 tablespoon maple-flavoured syrup
1 tablespoon brandy
⅓ cup (50g) plain flour

Combine butter, sugar and maple syrup in medium pan, stir over heat, without boiling, until sugar is dissolved, simmer, uncovered, without stirring, 2 minutes. Remove from heat, stir in brandy and flour. Drop level teaspoons of mixture onto greased oven trays; allow 4 per tray. Bake in moderate oven about 7 minutes or until lightly browned. Remove from oven; cool on tray 1 minute.

Lift tuiles from tray using metal spatula, gently pinch centres with fingers, cool over wooden spoon 1 minute before placing on wire rack to cool completely.
Makes about 25.

APRICOT GLAZED BUTTERSCOTCH SLICE

100g butter, chopped
¾ cup (150g) firmly packed
**   brown sugar**
2 tablespoons cream
1 cup (150g) plain flour
1 egg, lightly beaten
⅓ cup (55g) blanched almonds
2 tablespoons apricot jam, warmed

Grease 19cm x 29cm rectangular slice pan, place strip of foil to cover base and extend over 2 opposite sides.

Combine butter, sugar and cream in medium heavy-based pan, stir over heat, without boiling, until sugar is dissolved. Bring to boil, boil, uncovered, without stirring, about 3 minutes or until mixture becomes darker in colour; cool 10 minutes.

Stir flour and egg into mixture, spread into prepared pan, top with nuts. Bake in moderate oven about 20 minutes or until just firm. Brush warm slice with jam; cool slice in pan.

ABOVE: Maple Syrup Tuiles.
RIGHT: Apricot Glazed Butterscotch Slice.

Right: Box and serviette from Opus.

CARAMEL CHOCOLATE CREAM SLICE

250g packet Jersey caramels,
  chopped
100g white chocolate, chopped
¼ cup (60ml) cream
1 tablespoon light corn syrup
200g packet Tim Tams, chopped
100g White Melts, melted

Grease 23cm square slab cake pan, place strip of baking paper to cover base and extend over 2 opposite sides.

Combine caramels, chopped chocolate, cream and corn syrup in medium heatproof bowl, stir over pan of simmering water until smooth; gently stir in Tim Tams. Spread mixture into prepared pan; refrigerate until set. Cut into triangles, drizzle with White Melts.

CARAMEL PECAN COCONUT SLICE

½ cup (75g) plain flour
½ cup (75g) self-raising flour
¼ cup (55g) caster sugar
½ cup (45g) coconut
60g butter, melted
1 egg, lightly beaten

TOPPING
2 eggs, lightly beaten
½ teaspoon vanilla essence
⅔ cup (80g) chopped pecans, toasted
1 cup (200g) firmly packed
  brown sugar
½ teaspoon baking powder
125g Jersey caramels, chopped
¾ cup (65g) coconut

Grease 19cm x 29cm rectangular slice pan, place strip of baking paper to cover base and extend over 2 opposite sides.

Combine all ingredients in medium bowl; mix well. Press mixture over base of prepared pan. Bake in moderate oven about 15 minutes or until lightly browned. Spread topping over hot base, bake in moderate oven 25 minutes or until firm; cool in pan. Serve slice dusted with sifted icing sugar, if desired.

Topping: Combine all ingredients in medium bowl; mix well.

LEFT: Caramel Chocolate Cream Slice.
RIGHT: Caramel Pecan Coconut Slice.

Left: China from Home & Garden on the Mall.
Right: Basket and cloth from Pacific East India Co.

COCONUT CARAMEL SLICE

125g butter, chopped
½ cup (100g) firmly packed
  brown sugar
¾ cup (65g) coconut
1 cup (150g) plain flour
1 egg yolk
½ cup (60g) chopped pecans

FILLING
400g can sweetened condensed milk
60g butter
2 tablespoons golden syrup

TOPPING
60g butter, melted
1 tablespoon golden syrup
½ cup (45g) coconut
½ cup (35g) shredded coconut
½ cup (50g) crushed Weet-Bix

Process butter, sugar, coconut and flour until mixture resembles breadcrumbs. Add yolk and nuts, process until mixture forms a ball; press over base of greased 20cm x 30cm lamington pan. Bake in moderate oven about 20 minutes or until lightly browned. Spread hot filling over hot base, sprinkle with topping. Bake in moderate oven 15 minutes or until browned; cool in pan.

Filling: Combine all ingredients in medium heavy-based pan, stir over heat until mixture boils, simmer, stirring, about 8 minutes or until mixture is golden brown.

Topping: Combine all ingredients in medium bowl; mix well.

GOLDEN POPCORN NUGGETS

**250g packet Jersey caramels,
    chopped**
60g butter
2 tablespoons golden syrup
2 tablespoons light corn syrup
**1 cup (150g) unsalted roasted
    peanuts, chopped**
6 cups (85g) unsalted popped corn

Combine caramels, butter and both syrups in medium pan, stir over heat, without boiling, until mixture is smooth. Stir in peanuts and popcorn; mix well. Drop level tablespoons of mixture onto greased trays, shape into balls, using damp hands. Stand at room temperature until firm.

Makes about 40.

HONEYED BUTTERSCOTCH SEED BARS

1 cup (220g) caster sugar
1/2 cup (125ml) water
80g butter, chopped
1/4 cup (60ml) honey
1/2 cup (75g) sesame seeds, toasted
2 tablespoons pepitas, toasted
**2 tablespoons sunflower seed
    kernels, toasted**
**2 tablespoons coarsely chopped
    macadamias, toasted**

Grease 20cm x 30cm lamington pan, place strip of baking paper to cover base and extend over 2 opposite sides.

Combine sugar, water and butter in medium heavy-based pan, stir over heat, without boiling, until sugar is dissolved. Bring to boil, simmer, uncovered, shaking pan occasionally, until mixture is lightly browned. Remove from heat, quickly stir in remaining ingredients; pour into prepared pan. Stand about 5 minutes before marking into pieces. Cool in pan; break into pieces.

LEFT: Coconut Caramel Slice.
ABOVE LEFT: Golden Popcorn Nuggets.
RIGHT: Honeyed Butterscotch Seed Bars.

Left: Marble from Corso De' Fiori.

65

YOGURT SULTANA CHIP COOKIES

Chopped carob can be substituted for dark chocolate, if preferred.

125g butter, melted
1¼ cups (35g) Corn Flakes
1 cup (150g) self-raising flour
½ cup (100g) firmly packed brown sugar
½ cup (25g) flaked coconut
200g yogurt-coated sultanas
80g dark chocolate, chopped
⅔ cup (80g) chopped roasted hazelnuts
1 egg, lightly beaten

Combine all ingredients in large bowl; mix well. Roll level tablespoons of mixture into balls, place about 5cm apart on greased oven trays. Bake in moderate oven about 12 minutes or until browned; cool on trays.

Makes about 40.

CORNFLAKE CHOCOLATE JOYS

150g butter, chopped
⅓ cup (80ml) light corn syrup
3 cups (90g) Corn Flakes
3 x 40g Milo bars, chopped
½ cup (40g) flaked almonds, toasted
½ cup (45g) coconut
⅓ cup (85g) chopped glace cherries

Combine butter and corn syrup in large pan, stir over heat until butter is melted; cool 20 minutes. Gently stir in remaining ingredients. Drop rounded tablespoons of mixture into paper patty cases, place on tray. Refrigerate until set, sprinkle with a little extra Milo, if desired.

Makes about 20.

LEFT: Yogurt Sultana Chip Cookies.
ABOVE: Cornflake Chocolate Joys.

AFGHANS

Carob powder can be substituted for cocoa, if preferred.

200g butter, chopped
¾ cup (150g) firmly packed brown sugar
1 cup (150g) plain flour
¼ cup (25g) cocoa
2 cups (60g) Corn Flakes
½ cup (50g) crushed Weet-Bix
¼ cup (30g) chopped roasted hazelnuts

CHOCOLATE HAZELNUT FROSTING
60g packaged cream cheese, chopped
60g butter, chopped
2 tablespoons Nutella
1 cup (160g) icing sugar mixture

Beat butter and sugar in medium bowl with electric mixer until smooth. Stir in flour, cocoa, Corn Flakes and Weet-Bix; mix well. Drop rounded tablespoons of mixture about 5cm apart on greased oven trays; flatten slightly. Bake in moderately slow oven about 15 minutes or until browned; cool on trays. Spread biscuits with frosting; top with nuts.

Chocolate Hazelnut Frosting: Beat cheese, butter and Nutella in small bowl with electric mixer until light and fluffy, gradually beat in icing sugar.

Makes about 15.

FRUITY COCONUT OAT BARS

125g butter, melted
1 cup (90g) rolled oats
⅔ cup (110g) sultanas
½ cup (45g) coconut
¼ cup (60g) chopped glace apricots
½ cup (75g) self-raising flour
½ cup (110g) caster sugar
1 tablespoon honey
1 tablespoon golden syrup

Grease 23cm square slab cake pan, place strip of baking paper to cover base and extend over 2 opposite sides.

Combine all ingredients in large bowl; mix well. Press mixture into prepared pan, bake in moderate oven about 20 minutes or until browned. Cool in pan; refrigerate before cutting.

ABOVE: Afghans.
RIGHT: Fruity Coconut Oat Bars.

PEANUT BUBBLE BARS

125g butter, chopped
⅓ cup (80ml) light corn syrup
⅓ cup (85g) smooth peanut butter
½ cup (110g) caster sugar
2 cups (70g) Rice Bubbles
2 cups (90g) Coco Pops
1 cup (80g) flaked almonds, toasted

Grease 20cm x 30cm lamington pan, place strip of baking paper to cover base and extend over 2 opposite sides.

Combine butter, corn syrup, peanut butter and sugar in medium heavy-based pan, stir over heat, without boiling, until sugar is dissolved. Bring to boil, simmer gently, uncovered, without stirring, 5 minutes. Gently stir in remaining ingredients. Press mixture into prepared pan; refrigerate until firm.

ABOVE: Peanut Bubble Bars.
ABOVE RIGHT: Nutty Cornflake Chocolate Dreams.
RIGHT: Choc Chip Muesli Slice.

Above: Serviette from House & Garden on the Mall. Right: China from Villeroy & Boch.

NUTTY CORNFLAKE CHOCOLATE DREAMS

Melted carob can be substituted for Choc and Milk Melts, if preferred.

100g butter, melted
3 cups (90g) Corn Flakes
1 cup (260g) smooth peanut butter
1 cup (100g) milk powder
1 cup (160g) icing sugar mixture
1½ cups (225g) Choc Melts, melted
1½ cups (225g) Milk Melts, melted

Combine butter, Corn Flakes, peanut butter, milk powder and icing sugar in large bowl; mix well. Refrigerate mixture about 1 hour or until just firm.

Roll heaped teaspoons of mixture into balls, flatten slightly, place on foil-covered trays; refrigerate until firm. Dip half of each biscuit into Choc Melts, place on trays; refrigerate until set. Dip other half of biscuits into Milk Melts, place on trays; refrigerate until set. Store in refrigerator.

Makes about 45.

CHOC CHIP MUESLI SLICE

Carob powder and chopped carob can be substituted for cocoa and Choc Bits, if preferred.

125g butter, chopped
½ cup (100g) firmly packed
**   brown sugar**
¼ cup (60ml) honey
¾ cup (110g) self-raising flour
½ cup (75g) plain flour
2 tablespoons cocoa
1½ cups (165g) natural muesli
1 cup (190g) Choc Bits
½ cup (60g) chopped pecans
1 egg, lightly beaten

Grease 19cm x 29cm rectangular slice pan, place strip of foil to cover base and extend over 2 opposite sides.

Combine butter, sugar and honey in medium pan, stir over heat until butter is melted; cool 5 minutes. Stir in remaining ingredients; mix well. Spread mixture into prepared pan. Bake in moderate oven about 25 minutes or until firm; cool in pan. Serve slice dusted with sifted icing sugar, if desired.

CHOCOLATE OAT CREAMS

Roughly chopped carob can be substituted for Choc Melts, if preferred.

100g butter, chopped
¼ cup (60ml) golden syrup
2 cups (200g) quick cooking oats
½ cup (110g) raw sugar
¼ cup (35g) plain flour
CHOCOLATE FILLING
1 cup (150g) Choc Melts
¼ cup (60ml) cream

Combine butter and golden syrup in medium pan, stir over heat until butter is melted. Stir in remaining ingredients. Roll rounded teaspoons of mixture into balls, place about 3cm apart on ungreased oven trays; flatten until 1cm thick. Bake in moderate oven about 15 minutes or until browned. Loosen biscuits while warm; cool on trays. Sandwich biscuits with chocolate filling.

Chocolate Filling: Combine ingredients in small heatproof bowl, stir over pan of simmering water until smooth. Refrigerate about 1 hour or until spreadable.

Makes about 20.

CHOC MALT SULTANA COOKIES

250g butter, chopped
1 teaspoon vanilla essence
1 cup (200g) firmly packed brown sugar
2 tablespoons honey
2 eggs
2¼ cups (335g) plain flour
½ teaspoon baking powder
1½ cups (150g) quick cooking oats
½ cup (60g) instant malted milk powder
1 cup (200g) chocolate-coated sultanas

Beat butter, essence, sugar, honey and eggs in large bowl with electric mixer until smooth. Stir in remaining ingredients; mix well. Drop level tablespoons of mixture about 3cm apart onto baking paper-covered oven trays. Bake in moderately slow oven about 20 minutes or until browned; cool on trays.

Makes about 50.

ABOVE: Chocolate Oat Creams.
RIGHT: Choc Malt Sultana Cookies.

HAZELNUT CHOCOLATE SLICE

60g butter
½ cup (100g) firmly packed
brown sugar
½ cup (125ml) golden syrup
3 cups (105g) Rice Bubbles
½ cup (35g) shredded coconut
½ cup (125ml) Nutella
1 cup (125g) chopped roasted
hazelnuts

CHOCOLATE TOPPING
200g milk chocolate, chopped
¼ cup (60ml) cream

Grease 20cm x 30cm lamington pan, place strip of baking paper to cover base and extend over 2 opposite sides.

Combine butter, sugar and golden syrup in medium heavy-based pan, stir over heat, without boiling, until sugar is dissolved. Bring to boil, boil, uncovered, without stirring, 2 minutes. Stir in Rice Bubbles, coconut and Nutella. Press mixture into prepared pan, sprinkle with nuts. Spread with chocolate topping; refrigerate until firm.

Chocolate Topping: Combine chocolate and cream in heatproof bowl, stir over pan of simmering water until smooth.

APRICOT PEANUT OAT COOKIES

125g butter, chopped
⅓ cup (85g) smooth peanut butter
¾ cup (110g) self-raising flour
1 cup (90g) rolled oats
1 cup (150g) chopped dried apricots
1 cup (150g) chopped unsalted
roasted peanuts
¾ cup (120g) icing sugar mixture
1 egg, lightly beaten

Combine butter and peanut butter in medium pan, stir over heat until butter is melted. Remove from heat, stir in remaining ingredients; mix well. Drop level tablespoons of mixture about 3cm apart onto greased oven trays. Bake in moderate oven about 12 minutes or until browned; cool on trays.

Makes about 35.

LEFT: Hazelnut Chocolate Slice.
RIGHT: Apricot Peanut Oat Cookies.

Right: Plate and tray from Pacific East India Co.

GIANT CHOC OAT RAISIN COOKIES

125g butter, chopped
1 teaspoon vanilla essence
1 cup (200g) firmly packed
   brown sugar
½ cup (110g) caster sugar
2 tablespoons honey
2 eggs
1¾ cups (260g) plain flour
1 teaspoon bicarbonate of soda
1½ cups (135g) rolled oats
½ cup (85g) chopped raisins
½ cup (60g) chopped pecans,
   toasted
125g white chocolate, chopped

Beat butter, essence, sugars, honey and eggs in medium bowl with electric mixer until combined; stir in remaining ingredients. Roll ¼ cups (60ml) of mixture into balls, using floured hands. Place balls about 10cm apart on greased oven trays (allow 4 per tray); flatten until 1cm thick. Bake in moderate oven about 12 minutes or until lightly browned. Stand cookies 2 minutes before lifting onto wire racks to cool.

Makes about 16.

CHEWY PEANUT BUTTER BARS

60g butter, chopped
¼ cup (60ml) honey
½ cup (100g) firmly packed
   brown sugar
⅓ cup (85g) smooth peanut butter
2 tablespoons marmalade
1 cup (90g) rolled oats
1 cup (35g) Rice Bubbles
⅓ cup (35g) crushed Weet-Bix
½ cup (35g) shredded coconut
½ cup (75g) fruit medley
¼ cup (55g) finely chopped
   glace pineapple

Combine butter, honey, sugar, peanut butter and marmalade in large heavy-based pan, stir over low heat, without boiling, until sugar is dissolved. Bring to boil, remove from heat, stir in remaining ingredients; mix well. Press mixture firmly into greased 23cm square slab cake pan; refrigerate until firm.

ABOVE: Giant Choc Oat Raisin Cookies.
RIGHT: Chewy Peanut Butter Bars.

Above: Setting from Accoutrement. Right: Mug from Barbara's Storehouse.

FRUITY ALMOND PISTACHIO SLICE

¾ cup (180ml) sweetened condensed milk
125g butter, chopped
2 teaspoons grated lemon rind
1½ cups (150g) plain sweet biscuit crumbs
½ cup (125g) chopped red glace cherries
½ cup (150g) chopped glace figs
½ cup (125g) chopped glace peaches
⅓ cup (55g) chopped almond kernels, toasted
⅓ cup (50g) chopped pistachios, toasted
¾ cup (65g) coconut
100g dark chocolate, melted
60g butter, melted, extra
1 tablespoon chopped almond kernels, extra
1 tablespoon chopped pistachios, extra

Grease 19cm x 29cm rectangular slice pan, place strip of baking paper to cover base and extend over 2 opposite sides.

Combine milk, butter and rind in medium pan, stir over heat until butter is melted. Add crumbs, fruit, nuts and coconut; mix well. Press mixture evenly over base of prepared pan. Spread with combined chocolate and extra butter, sprinkle with extra nuts; refrigerate until set.

FRUITCAKE COOKIES

100g butter, chopped
¾ cup (150g) firmly packed brown sugar
2 tablespoons molasses
1 teaspoon dark rum, brandy or sweet sherry
1 egg
1 cup (150g) plain flour
¼ teaspoon baking powder
½ cup (45g) rolled oats
½ cup (60g) chopped pecans
¼ cup (40g) chopped blanched almonds
1 cup (190g) mixed dried fruit

Beat butter, sugar, molasses, rum and egg in small bowl with electric mixer until smooth. Stir in remaining ingredients in 2 batches. Drop level tablespoons of mixture about 5cm apart onto greased oven trays, bake in moderate oven about 15 minutes or until browned. Stand 5 minutes before lifting onto wire racks to cool.

Makes about 35.

BELOW: Fruitcake Cookies.
RIGHT: Fruity Almond Pistachio Slice.

SPICY FRUIT AND CARROT SLICE

You will need 1 large (180g) carrot.

90g butter, chopped
1/3 cup (75g) caster sugar
1 egg yolk
3/4 cup (105g) plain flour
2 tablespoons self-raising flour
2 tablespoons coconut

TOPPING
2 tablespoons chopped
   seedless prunes
2 tablespoons sultanas
1/4 cup (30g) chopped walnuts,
   toasted
1/2 cup (75g) self-raising flour
1 teaspoon ground cinnamon
1/2 teaspoon ground ginger
1/4 teaspoon ground nutmeg
3/4 cup (130g) firmly packed
   finely grated carrot
1 egg, lightly beaten
1/3 cup (80ml) vegetable oil
1/2 teaspoon bicarbonate of soda
1/2 cup (100g) firmly packed
   brown sugar
1/4 cup (35g) finely chopped
   dried pears

Grease 19cm x 29cm rectangular slice pan, place strip of baking paper to cover base and extend over 2 opposite sides.

Beat butter, sugar and yolk in small bowl with electric mixer until smooth. Stir in flours and coconut, press evenly over base of prepared pan. Bake in moderate oven about 20 minutes or until browned; cool. Spread topping over base, bake in moderately slow oven about 35 minutes or until slice is firm; cool in pan.
Topping: Combine all ingredients in medium bowl; mix well.

CHEWY GINGER BANANA COOKIES

You will need about 1 medium (200g) over-ripe banana for this recipe.

125g butter, chopped
1 teaspoon grated lemon rind
1 cup (200g) firmly packed
   brown sugar
1 egg yolk
1/3 cup mashed over-ripe banana
1/2 cup (60g) chopped walnuts
2 cups (300g) plain flour
1 tablespoon ground ginger
1/2 teaspoon bicarbonate of soda

Beat butter, rind, sugar and yolk in small bowl with electric mixer until smooth. Stir in remaining ingredients. Drop rounded teaspoons of mixture about 5cm apart onto greased oven trays. Bake in moderate oven about 12 minutes or until firm; cool on wire racks.

Makes 65.

LEFT: Spicy Fruit and Carrot Slice.
RIGHT: Chewy Ginger Banana Cookies.

LEMON CURRANT COOKIES

150g butter, chopped
1 teaspoon grated lemon rind
½ cup (100g) firmly packed brown sugar
1 cup (150g) self-raising flour
¼ cup (35g) plain flour
¼ cup (35g) dried currants

Beat butter, rind and sugar in small bowl with electric mixer until smooth. Stir in flours and currants. Roll rounded teaspoons of mixture into balls, place about 5cm apart on greased oven trays, flatten slightly with a floured fork. Bake in slow oven about 20 minutes or until lightly browned. Stand 5 minutes before lifting onto wire racks to cool.

Makes about 40.

LIME CHEESECAKE SLICE

450g rectangular piece of madeira cake
500g packaged cream cheese, softened
2 teaspoons grated lime rind
3 teaspoons gelatine
¼ cup (60ml) lime juice
¼ cup (55g) caster sugar
1 tablespoon honey
½ cup (125ml) buttermilk
½ cup (125ml) cream

Grease 20cm x 30cm lamington pan; line base and sides with plastic wrap.

Cut browned part of cake away, cut cake into 4 even slices. Place cake in a single layer in prepared pan; trim to fit.

Beat cheese and rind in large bowl with electric mixer until smooth. Sprinkle gelatine over juice in cup, stand in small pan of simmering water, stir until dissolved. Add gelatine mixture, sugar, honey, buttermilk and cream to cream cheese mixture; beat until combined. Pour mixture over prepared base; refrigerate until set.

ABOVE: Lemon Currant Cookies.
RIGHT: Lime Cheesecake Slice.

Above: Setting from Accoutrement.

RASPBERRY ALMOND SLICE

1 cup (150g) self-raising flour
1 cup (150g) plain flour
1½ cups (300g) firmly packed
**   brown sugar**
125g butter, chopped
1 teaspoon bicarbonate of soda
¾ cup (180ml) buttermilk
1 egg, lightly beaten
2 teaspoons grated lemon rind
125g fresh or frozen raspberries
¼ cup (20g) flaked almonds

Process flours, sugar and butter until mixture resembles breadcrumbs. Press 2 cups of the mixture over base of greased 20cm x 30cm lamington pan. Stir soda, buttermilk, egg and rind into remaining mixture; mix well. Pour over base, top with berries, sprinkle with nuts. Bake in moderate oven about 35 minutes or until firm; cool in pan.

FRUIT AND NUT CHOC CHIP COOKIES

Chopped carob can be substituted for Choc Bits, if preferred.

125g butter, chopped
½ cup (100g) firmly packed
**   brown sugar**
1 egg
1½ cups (225g) self-raising flour
¼ cup (20g) rolled oats
½ cup (85g) chopped seedless dates
½ cup (60g) chopped pecans, toasted
½ cup (95g) Choc Bits

Beat butter, sugar and egg in small bowl with electric mixer until smooth. Stir in remaining ingredients; mix well. Roll level tablespoons of mixture into balls, place about 5cm apart on greased oven trays, flatten slightly with a floured fork. Bake in moderate oven about 15 minutes or until browned. Stand 5 minutes before lifting onto wire racks to cool.

Makes about 30.

LEFT: Raspberry Almond Slice.
RIGHT: Fruit and Nut Choc Chip Cookies.

Left: Box from Opus. Right: Box from Barbara's Storehouse.

MACADAMIA DATE SLICE

125g butter, chopped
¾ cup (150g) firmly packed
   brown sugar
1 egg
1 tablespoon maple-flavoured syrup
1 cup (150g) plain flour
½ teaspoon baking powder
¼ teaspoon ground ginger
½ cup (75g) chopped macadamias
½ cup (80g) chopped seedless dates
¼ cup (35g) dried currants
¼ cup (10g) flaked coconut

Grease 23cm square slab cake pan, place strip of foil to cover base and extend over 2 opposite sides.

Beat butter, sugar, egg and maple syrup in small bowl with electric mixer until smooth. Beat in flour, baking powder and ginger in 3 batches on low speed until combined. Stir in remaining ingredients. Spread mixture into prepared pan, bake in moderate oven about 20 minutes or until browned; cool in pan.

FRUIT MINCE SURPRISES

1 cup (150g) white self-raising flour
½ cup (80g) wholemeal plain flour
2 tablespoons wheatgerm
¼ cup (55g) caster sugar
¼ cup (50g) firmly packed
   brown sugar
1 teaspoon ground cinnamon
100g butter, chopped
1 egg
1 teaspoon water, approximately
½ cup (125ml) fruit mince

Process flours, wheatgerm, sugars, cinnamon and butter until mixture resembles breadcrumbs. Add egg and enough water to make ingredients cling together. Knead dough on lightly floured surface until smooth; cover, refrigerate dough 30 minutes.

Roll dough between sheets of baking paper until 4mm thick, cut into 7.5cm rounds; re-roll pastry as necessary. Drop a level teaspoon of fruit mince onto centre of each round, brush edges lightly with water. Gently pinch edges together to enclose filling, place about 3cm apart, seam side down, on greased oven trays; flatten slightly. Bake in moderate oven about 20 minutes or until lightly browned; cool on wire racks. Serve dusted with sifted icing sugar, if desired.

Makes about 24.

LEFT: Fruit Mince Surprises.
ABOVE: Macadamia Date Slice.

LEMON PASSIONFRUIT SLICE

You will need about 3 passionfruit for this recipe.

150g butter, melted
**250g packet plain sweet
    biscuits, crushed**
¼ cup (20g) coconut
250g packet cream cheese, softened
2 teaspoons grated lemon rind
⅓ cup (75g) caster sugar
2 eggs
1 tablespoon lemon juice

PASSIONFRUIT TOPPING
300ml sour cream
¼ cup (60ml) passionfruit pulp
**¼ cup (50g) firmly packed
    brown sugar**

Grease 20cm x 30cm lamington pan, place strip of foil to cover base and extend over 2 opposite sides.

Combine butter, crumbs and coconut in small bowl; mix well. Press mixture over base of prepared pan; refrigerate 30 minutes.

Beat cheese, rind and sugar in small bowl with electric mixer until smooth. Add eggs 1 at a time, beat well between additions, beat in juice. Pour mixture over biscuit base, bake in moderately slow oven about 30 minutes or until just set. Spread hot cheesecake evenly with passionfruit topping, bake further 20 minutes; cool in oven with door ajar. Refrigerate overnight.

Passionfruit Topping: Combine all ingredients in small bowl; mix well.

BELOW: Lemon Passionfruit Slice.
RIGHT: Fruity Maple Cornflake Slice.

Right: Table and tray from FX Designs; coffee set from Ventura Designs.

FRUITY MAPLE CORNFLAKE SLICE

1 cup (250ml) cream
⅓ cup (80ml) maple-flavoured syrup
**⅔ cup (130g) firmly packed
    brown sugar**
20g butter
4 cups (120g) Corn Flakes
½ cup (40g) flaked almonds, toasted
½ cup (35g) shredded coconut
½ cup (75g) chopped dried pears
½ cup (45g) chopped dried apples

Combine cream, maple syrup, sugar and butter in medium heavy-based pan, stir over low heat, without boiling, until sugar is dissolved. Bring to boil, boil, uncovered, without stirring, about 10 minutes or until mixture is thickened. Stir in remaining ingredients; mix well. Press mixture into greased 20cm x 30cm lamington pan; cool. Refrigerate until firm.

WHEATMEAL APRICOT COCONUT SLICE

250g packet Shredded Wheatmeal biscuits
125g butter, melted
½ cup (125ml) light corn syrup
2 tablespoons coconut

FILLING
1⅔ cups (250g) dried apricots
1½ cups (135g) coconut
½ cup (70g) slivered almonds
400g can sweetened condensed milk
¼ cup (60ml) cream
1 tablespoon caster sugar
1 teaspoon grated lemon rind

Grease 20cm x 30cm lamington pan, place strip of baking paper to cover base and extend over 2 opposite sides.

Process biscuits until finely crushed, add butter and corn syrup, process until combined. Press biscuit mixture over base of prepared pan; refrigerate 10 minutes. Spread filling evenly over biscuit base, sprinkle with coconut, refrigerate until firm.
Filling: Process apricots, coconut and nuts until finely chopped. Add milk, cream, sugar and rind; process until combined.

BELOW: Apricot Crumble Slice.
RIGHT: Wheatmeal Apricot Coconut Slice.

Below: Setting from Prima Cosa. Right: Plate from Corso De' Fiori.

APRICOT CRUMBLE SLICE

90g butter, melted
1 cup (150g) plain flour
⅓ cup (75g) caster sugar

FILLING
1⅔ cups (250g) finely chopped dried apricots
1 cup (250ml) water
¼ cup (55g) caster sugar

COCONUT TOPPING
90g butter, melted
⅓ cup (30g) coconut
¼ cup (15g) shredded coconut
½ cup (75g) plain flour
½ cup (100g) firmly packed brown sugar

Combine butter, flour and sugar in small bowl; press mixture over base of greased 19cm x 29cm rectangular slice pan. Bake in moderate oven about 20 minutes or until browned. Spread hot filling over hot base, sprinkle with coconut topping. Bake in moderate oven about 20 minutes or until browned; cool in pan.
Filling: Combine apricots, water and sugar in medium heavy-based pan, simmer, uncovered, about 10 minutes or until thick, stirring occasionally.
Coconut Topping: Combine all ingredients in medium bowl; mix well.

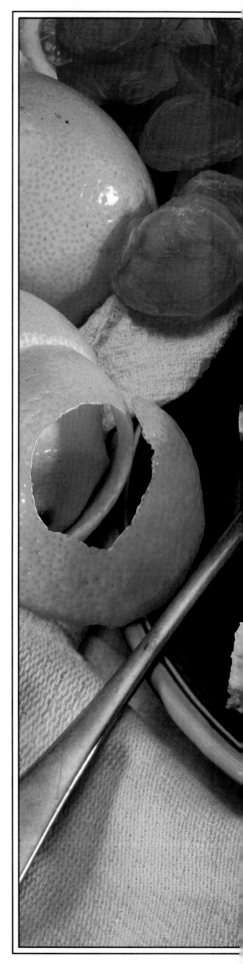

FIG AND DATE ROLLS

125g butter, chopped
⅓ cup (75g) caster sugar
1 teaspoon ground cinnamon
1 egg
½ cup (60g) packaged
    ground almonds
1⅓ cups (200g) plain flour

FILLING
1¾ cups (310g) finely chopped
    dried figs
½ cup (80g) finely chopped
    seedless dates
½ cup (125ml) water
2 teaspoons grated lemon rind
½ cup (110g) caster sugar

Beat butter, sugar, cinnamon and egg in medium bowl with electric mixer until smooth. Stir in nuts and flour, turn dough onto floured surface, divide dough into 4 portions. Cover; refrigerate 30 minutes.

Roll each portion of dough between sheets of lightly floured baking paper to 10cm x 20cm rectangle. Spread ½ cup of the filling along each rectangle, leaving 1cm border. Using the paper as a guide, fold long sides over filling to meet in the centre, gently press joins together, tuck ends under. Place rolls, seam side down, on greased oven trays. Bake in moderate oven about 25 minutes or until lightly browned; cool on trays. Cut into 1.5cm slices when cold.

Filling: Combine all ingredients in medium heavy-based pan, stir over heat, without boiling, until sugar is dissolved. Simmer, uncovered, about 15 minutes or until mixture is thick and pulpy, stirring occasionally; cool.

Makes about 25.

APPLE COCONUT CREAM SLICE

140g butter, melted
340g packet Golden Buttercake mix
1 cup (90g) coconut
425g can pie apple
½ cup (125ml) sour cream
1 egg
1 tablespoon cinnamon sugar
½ cup (40g) flaked almonds

Grease 23cm square slab cake pan, place strip of baking paper to cover base and extend over 2 opposite sides.

Combine butter, cake mix and coconut in large bowl; mix well. Press over base of prepared pan, bake in moderate oven about 12 minutes or until lightly browned; cool 5 minutes.

Combine pie apple, cream, egg and sugar in medium bowl; mix well. Spread mixture over base, sprinkle with nuts. Bake in moderate oven about 40 minutes or until browned; cool in pan.

LEFT: Fig and Date Rolls.
ABOVE: Apple Coconut Cream Slice.

Left: China from Waterford Wedgwood.

NUTTY CHOCAROONS

Melted carob can be substituted for dark chocolate, if preferred.

2 egg whites
¾ cup (165g) caster sugar
¾ cup (120g) finely chopped toasted Brazil nuts
⅔ cup (60g) coconut
250g dark chocolate, melted

Beat egg whites in small bowl with electric mixer until soft peaks form. Gradually add sugar, beating until dissolved between additions. Fold in nuts and coconut. Drop rounded teaspoons of mixture about 5cm apart onto greased oven trays. Bake in moderate oven about 15 minutes or until lightly browned. Stand 5 minutes before lifting onto wire racks to cool.

Dip the base of each macaroon in chocolate, place on baking paper-covered trays to set. Spoon remaining chocolate into small piping bag fitted with small plain tube; drizzle over macaroons.

Makes about 50.

COFFEE MALT SURPRISE SLICE

200g packet Coffee Eclairs
1 tablespoon cream
1 cup (35g) Rice Bubbles
100g packet raspberry marshmallows, chopped
165g packet Maltesers

Combine Eclairs and cream in medium heavy-based pan, stir over low heat until smooth. Remove from heat, stir in Rice Bubbles and marshmallows; quickly stir in Maltesers. Press mixture lightly into greased 8cm x 26cm bar cake pan; refrigerate until set. Cut with a serrated knife.

ABOVE: Coffee Malt Surprise Slice.
RIGHT: Nutty Chocaroons.

Right: China by Mikasa; tableware from David Jones.

MILK CHOCOLATE BUBBLE SLICE

125g butter, chopped
200g milk chocolate, chopped
6 x 25g Milky Way bars, chopped
2 cups (70g) Rice Bubbles
½ cup (45g) coconut
150g packet coconut
    macaroons, chopped
¼ cup (60ml) sour cream
⅔ cup (100g) Choc Melts, melted

Grease 23cm square slab cake pan, place strip of baking paper to cover base and extend over 2 opposite sides.

Combine butter, chocolate and half the Milky Way bars in medium heavy-based pan, stir over low heat until mixture is just melted. Remove from heat, stir in Rice Bubbles, coconut, macaroons and sour cream; mix well. Stir in remaining Milky Way bars. Press firmly into prepared pan. Drizzle with Choc Melts; refrigerate until set.

HONEYED CORN CUPS

Unflavoured popcorn can be substituted for puffed corn, if preferred.

100g packet Mallow Bakes
125g butter, chopped
¾ cup (150g) firmly packed
    brown sugar
¼ cup (60ml) tahini
2 tablespoons honey
2 cups (260g) toasted muesli
2 cups (45g) puffed corn, toasted

Reserve ½ cup (25g) Mallow Bakes. Combine butter, sugar, tahini and honey in large heavy-based pan, stir over low heat until butter is melted; cool 10 minutes. Stir in remaining Mallow Bakes, muesli and corn; mix well. Drop rounded tablespoons of mixture into paper patty cases, top with reserved Mallow Bakes, place on trays; refrigerate until set.

Makes about 24.

LEFT: Milk Chocolate Bubble Slice.
ABOVE: Honeyed Corn Cups.

Left: Plate and straw placemat from Barbara's Storehouse. Above: Sugar and cream set from Barbara's Storehouse.

PEANUT BUTTER MALLOW SLICE

Finely chopped carob can be substituted for Milk Melts, if preferred.

40g butter, chopped
250g white marshmallows
½ cup (130g) smooth peanut butter
2½ cups (85g) Rice Bubbles
½ cup (75g) dried currants

TOPPING
¼ cup (65g) smooth peanut butter
1 cup (150g) Milk Melts
50g white marshmallows, quartered

Grease 19cm x 29cm rectangular slice pan, place strip of baking paper to cover base and extend over 2 opposite sides.

Combine butter, marshmallows and peanut butter in medium heavy-based pan, stir constantly over low heat until marshmallows are melted. Stir in Rice Bubbles and currants; mix well. Press into prepared pan, using wet fingers. Spread with warm topping, refrigerate until set.
Topping: Combine all ingredients in heatproof bowl, stir over pan of simmering water until smooth.

MOCHA FUDGE MALLOW SLICE

Chopped carob can be substituted for milk chocolate, if preferred.

250g packet Butternut Cookies
100g butter, melted

FILLING
2 tablespoons caster sugar
60g butter, chopped
½ cup (125ml) cream
1 tablespoon dry instant coffee
2 x 100g packets white marshmallows, halved
200g milk chocolate, chopped

Grease 23cm square slab cake pan, place strip of baking paper to cover base and extend over 2 opposite sides.

Process cookies until finely crushed, add butter, process until combined. Press mixture over base of prepared pan; refrigerate 10 minutes.

Pour warm filling over base in pan; refrigerate until set. Cut with a knife dipped in hot water. Store in refrigerator.
Filling: Combine all ingredients in medium heavy-based pan, stir over low heat until mixture is smooth.

LEFT: Peanut Butter Mallow Slice.
RIGHT: Mocha Fudge Mallow Slice.

Right: Tapestry and fleur-de-lis serviette rings from Home & Garden on the Mall.

LEMON CREAM CHEESE SLICE

**2 x 150g packets coconut
    macaroons, crushed**
140g butter, melted
2 tablespoons honey

FILLING
3 teaspoons gelatine
¼ cup (60ml) water
**500g packaged cream cheese
    softened, chopped**
280g jar lemon butter
½ cup (125ml) sour cream

Grease 20cm x 30cm lamington pan, place strip of baking paper to cover base and extend over 2 opposite sides.

Combine macaroons, butter and honey in medium bowl; mix well. Press into prepared pan, roughen surface using a fork. Pour filling over macaroon base; refrigerate until firm.

Filling: Sprinkle gelatine over water in cup, stand in small pan of simmering water, stir until dissolved. Beat cheese in medium bowl with electric mixer until smooth. Add gelatine mixture and remaining ingredients, beat until smooth.

MERINGUE CRITTERS

It is normal for meringues to crack a little during cooking.

4 egg whites
1 cup (220g) caster sugar
red food colouring
green food colouring
licorice
hundreds and thousands
assorted sweets to decorate

Cover greased oven trays with baking paper. Beat egg whites in small bowl with electric mixer until soft peaks form. Gradually add sugar, beating until dissolved between additions. Continue beating on high speed about 10 minutes or until firm peaks form.

Divide mixture into 2 portions. Add a few drops of red food colouring to 1 portion; mix well. Add a few drops of green food colouring to remaining portion; mix well. Pipe all critters about 5cm apart onto prepared trays. Decorate with licorice and sweets.

For ladybirds: Spoon red mixture into piping bag fitted with 12mm plain tube, pipe 8 x 4cm rounds, then smaller rounds, about 1.5cm, joining first round.

For spiders: Pipe 2 rounds, as for the ladybirds, but make first round slightly smaller.

For caterpillars: Spoon green mixture into clean piping bag fitted with 12mm plain tube. Pipe caterpillars in a spiral about 8cm long.

For bees: Pipe 3 rounds all joining each other, making each round progressively smaller than the first.

Bake critters in very slow oven about 45 minutes or until critters are dry to touch. Turn oven off, cool critters in oven.

Makes about 30.

ABOVE: Lemon Cream Cheese Slice.
RIGHT: Meringue Critters.

Right: Bunny from Pacific East India Co.

NUTTY GINGER MARMALADE FRUIT SLICE

¾ cup (125g) chopped raisins
¾ cup (120g) sultanas
½ cup (75g) quartered dried apricots
2 tablespoons boiling water
1¼ cups (310ml) ginger marmalade
¾ cup (120g) chopped
  almond kernels
¾ cup (90g) chopped pecans
2 teaspoons grated orange rind
2 eggs, lightly beaten
⅓ cup (50g) plain flour
¾ cup (105g) self-raising flour
1 cup (125g) packaged
  ground almonds
60g butter, melted
⅔ cup (130g) firmly packed
  brown sugar

Grease 26cm x 32cm Swiss roll pan, place strip of baking paper to cover base and extend over 2 opposite sides.

Combine raisins, sultanas, apricots and water in large bowl, cover; stand 5 minutes. Add remaining ingredients to fruit mixture; mix well; spread into prepared pan. Bake in moderate oven about 40 minutes or until browned. Turn onto wire rack to cool.

CITRUS CREAM CLOUDS

185g butter, chopped
1 teaspoon grated lime rind
½ cup (80g) icing sugar mixture
1⅓ cups (200g) plain flour
⅓ cup (40g) custard powder
2 teaspoons ground ginger
2 teaspoons lime juice

CITRUS CREAM
100g butter, chopped
1 teaspoon vanilla essence
1 teaspoon grated orange rind
1 cup (160g) icing sugar mixture
2 teaspoons lemon juice

Beat butter, rind and icing sugar in small bowl with electric mixer until smooth. Stir in remaining ingredients. Knead dough on lightly floured surface until smooth, cover; refrigerate 30 minutes.

Roll half the dough between sheets of baking paper until 3mm thick, cut out 30 x 4cm shapes. Roll scraps of dough with remaining half of dough until 3mm thick, cut out 30 x 6cm shapes. Place shapes about 2cm apart on greased oven trays. Bake in moderate oven about 8 minutes for smaller shapes, about 12 minutes for larger shapes, or until lightly browned. Lift onto wire racks to cool. Spoon citrus cream into piping bag fitted with small fluted tube. Pipe around edge and in centre of large biscuits, top with smaller biscuits. Dust with sifted icing sugar, if desired.

Citrus Cream: Beat butter, essence and rind in small bowl with electric mixer until light and fluffy. Gradually beat in icing sugar and juice.

Makes 30.

ABOVE: Nutty Ginger Marmalade Fruit Slice.
RIGHT: Citrus Cream Clouds.

Above: Plate from The Bay Tree Kitchen Shop; tapestry from Home & Garden on the Mall.

BLACK SUGAR AND GINGER SNAPS

1 cup (200g) firmly packed black sugar
3 teaspoons ground ginger
2 tablespoons finely chopped glace ginger
2 cups (300g) plain flour
200g butter, chopped
1 egg

Process sugar, gingers, flour and butter until mixture resembles breadcrumbs. Add egg, process until mixture forms a ball. Turn dough onto lightly floured surface, knead gently until smooth. Roll rounded teaspoons of mixture into balls, place about 5cm apart on greased oven trays, flatten slightly with a floured fork. Bake in moderately slow oven about 25 minutes or until browned.

Makes about 60.

FREEZE 'N' BAKE CHOC NUT COOKIES

Unbaked cookies can be kept in the freezer for up to 3 months. Chopped carob can be substituted for dark chocolate, if preferred.

185g butter, chopped
½ teaspoon vanilla essence
½ cup (100g) firmly packed brown sugar
½ cup (110g) caster sugar
1 egg
1¼ cups (185g) plain flour
½ cup (75g) self-raising flour
2 tablespoons chopped glace ginger
½ cup (60g) chopped pecans
100g dark chocolate, chopped

Beat butter, essence, sugars and egg in medium bowl with electric mixer until smooth. Stir in flours, ginger, nuts and chocolate in 2 batches. Place level tablespoons of mixture on foil-covered trays; freeze several hours or until firm. Transfer cookies to a plastic bag, seal tightly, store in freezer.

To bake, place frozen cookies about 3cm apart on greased oven tray, bake in moderately hot oven about 15 minutes or until browned; cool on tray.

Makes about 45.

LEFT: Black Sugar and Ginger Snaps.
BELOW: Freeze 'n' Bake Choc Nut Cookies.

HONEY MUNCHIES

½ cup (75g) plain flour
½ cup (75g) self-raising flour
¼ cup (50g) firmly packed
   brown sugar
¼ cup (35g) dried currants
2 teaspoons ground ginger
1 teaspoon ground cinnamon
1 teaspoon mixed spice
60g butter, chopped
2 tablespoons honey
1 teaspoon lemon juice,
   approximately

Process flours, sugar, currants, spices and butter until currants are finely chopped. Add honey, process with enough juice to make ingredients cling together. Knead on lightly floured surface until smooth, cover; refrigerate 30 minutes.

Roll dough between sheets of baking paper until 4mm thick. Using a 5cm gingerbread man cutter, cut out biscuits, place about 3cm apart on greased oven trays. Bake in moderate oven about 8 minutes or until browned; cool on wire racks.

Makes about 60.

HONEY BUMBLES

60g butter
⅓ cup (65g) firmly packed
   brown sugar
½ cup (125ml) honey
2 tablespoons molasses
2 cups (300g) self-raising flour
2 teaspoons mixed spice
½ teaspoon ground nutmeg
½ teaspoon ground cloves
¼ cup (40g) blanched almonds,
   approximately

Combine butter, sugar, honey and molasses in medium heavy-based pan, stir over heat until butter is melted; cool 5 minutes. Stir in flour and spices. Roll rounded teaspoons of mixture into balls, place about 5cm apart on greased oven trays, top with nuts. Bake in moderate oven about 15 minutes or until browned; cool on wire racks.

Makes about 45.

ABOVE: Honey Munchies.
RIGHT: Honey Bumbles.

Right: Fabric from Art House.

ANISE MARMALADE CRESCENTS

1¼ cups (185g) plain flour
⅓ cup (65g) firmly packed
brown sugar
¼ cup (35g) sesame seeds, toasted
¼ cup (25g) packaged ground
hazelnuts
1 teaspoon ground anise
1 teaspoon ground ginger
60g butter, chopped
1 egg yolk
1½ tablespoons marmalade
2 teaspoons cold water,
approximately

Process flour, sugar, seeds, nuts, spices and butter until ingredients are mixed. Add yolk, marmalade and enough water to mix to a soft dough. Knead dough on lightly floured surface until smooth; cover, refrigerate 30 minutes.

Roll dough between sheets of baking paper until 3mm thick. Cut 6.5cm crescents from dough, place about 2cm apart on greased oven trays, press diagonally with a floured fork. Bake in moderate oven about 10 minutes or until lightly browned. Lift onto wire racks to cool. Serve dusted with sifted icing sugar, if desired.

Makes about 50.

CARDAMOM GINGER CRISPS

125g butter, chopped
⅔ cup (130g) firmly packed
brown sugar
1 teaspoon ground cardamom
½ teaspoon ground cinnamon
pinch ground nutmeg
pinch ground cloves
2 egg yolks
1½ cups (225g) plain flour
2 tablespoons finely chopped
glace ginger

Beat butter, sugar, spices and yolks in small bowl with electric mixer until smooth. Stir in flour and glace ginger. Turn dough onto floured surface, knead until smooth. Shape dough into 7cm x 28cm rectangle, place on baking paper-covered tray; refrigerate 30 minutes.

Cut dough into 3mm slices, place about 3cm apart on baking paper-covered oven trays. Bake in moderately slow oven about 15 minutes or until golden brown; cool on wire racks.

Makes about 60.

LEFT: Anise Marmalade Crescents.
ABOVE: Cardamom Ginger Crisps.

GOLDEN CINNAMON BISCUITS

60g butter
⅓ cup (80ml) golden syrup
2 tablespoons brown sugar
2 tablespoons caster sugar
1½ cups (225g) self-raising flour
3 teaspoons ground cinnamon

Combine butter, golden syrup and sugars in medium heavy-based pan, stir over low heat until butter is melted; cool 5 minutes. Stir in flour and cinnamon. Roll rounded teaspoons of mixture into balls, place about 2cm apart on greased oven trays, flatten with a floured fork until 1cm thick. Bake in hot oven about 12 minutes or until browned. Stand 1 minute before lifting onto wire racks to cool.

Makes about 30.

GINGERED MARZIPAN CHOCOLATES

Melted carob can be substituted for dark chocolate, if preferred.

2 x 200g packets marzipan
¾ cup (150g) finely chopped
    crystallised ginger
250g dark chocolate, melted
1 tablespoon vegetable oil

Combine marzipan and ginger in bowl, knead until combined. Roll marzipan mixture between sheets of baking paper until 5mm thick, dust lightly with sifted icing sugar to prevent sticking. Cut marzipan mixture into 4cm rounds, dip rounds in combined chocolate and oil, place on baking paper-covered trays; refrigerate until set. Dust with sifted drinking chocolate, if desired.

Makes about 40.

LEFT: Golden Cinnamon Biscuits.
RIGHT: Gingered Marzipan Chocolates.

MINI CHOC TURNOVERS

Finely grated carob can be substituted for dark chocolate, if preferred.

1¼ cups (185g) plain flour
2 tablespoons caster sugar
1 teaspoon mixed spice
1 teaspoon ground cinnamon
1 teaspoon grated lemon rind
90g butter, chopped
1 egg, separated
2 tablespoons milk, approximately

FILLING
½ cup (100g) ricotta cheese
50g dark chocolate, finely grated
1 tablespoon caster sugar

Process flour, sugar, spices, rind and butter until mixture resembles breadcrumbs. Add yolk and enough milk to make ingredients cling together. Press dough into a ball, knead gently on lightly floured surface until smooth. Cover; refrigerate 15 minutes.

Roll half the dough on floured surface until 3mm thick; cut into 8cm rounds. Repeat with remaining dough. Place 1 level teaspoon of filling in centre of each round; brush edges of rounds with egg white, fold in half to enclose filling. Place turnovers about 2cm apart on greased oven trays. Bake in moderate oven about 15 minutes or until firm; cool on wire racks. Dust with icing sugar, if desired.
Filling: Combine all ingredients in bowl; mix well.

Makes about 20.

MAPLE CINNAMON PINWHEELS

2 cups (300g) plain flour
185g butter, chopped
½ cup (100g) firmly packed
   brown sugar
1 egg yolk
2 tablespoons maple-flavoured syrup

FILLING
¼ cup (60ml) maple-flavoured syrup
⅓ cup (40g) finely chopped
   walnuts, toasted
3 teaspoons cinnamon sugar

Process flour, butter and sugar until mixture resembles breadcrumbs. Add yolk and maple syrup, process until mixture forms a ball. Knead dough on lightly floured surface until smooth; cover, refrigerate 1 hour.

Roll dough between sheets of baking paper to 28cm x 48cm rectangle; spread filling evenly over dough, leaving 1cm border. Using paper as a guide, roll dough tightly from long side to enclose filling, wrap roll in plastic wrap, refrigerate 30 minutes.

Remove plastic from roll, cut roll into 1cm slices. Place slices about 2cm apart on greased oven trays. Bake in moderate oven about 15 minutes or until browned. Stand 5 minutes before lifting onto wire racks to cool.
Filling: Combine all ingredients in bowl; mix well.

Makes about 50.

LEFT: Mini Choc Turnovers.
RIGHT: Maple Cinnamon Pinwheels.

Right: China from David Jones.

RICH BLUE CHEESE AND POPPYSEED BISCUITS

1 cup (150g) plain flour
100g butter, chopped
75g mild full fat soft blue
  cheese, chopped
1½ tablespoons poppyseeds
sea salt

Process flour, butter and cheese until mixture forms a soft ball. Place mixture on plastic wrap and shape into a log 4cm in diameter; refrigerate until firm.

Remove log from plastic, roll in seeds, cut into 5mm slices. Place rounds about 3cm apart on ungreased oven trays, sprinkle with a little salt. Bake in moderately hot oven about 15 minutes or until lightly browned; cool on trays.

Makes about 30.

SPICY CHEESE SHAPES

Seasonings such as celery salt, lemon pepper, seasoned pepper, Szechwan pepper or garlic pepper, etc., can be sprinkled onto these biscuits.

1¼ cups (185g) plain flour
60g butter
1 egg yolk
½ cup (60g) finely grated tasty
  cheddar cheese
2 tablespoons milk, approximately
seasoning of your choice

Add flour to medium bowl, rub in butter. Add yolk, cheese and enough milk to make ingredients just cling together. Press mixture into a ball. Knead dough on lightly floured surface until smooth, cover; refrigerate 30 minutes.

Roll dough between sheets of baking paper until 3mm thick, cut into 5cm rounds and 4cm squares. Place shapes about 1cm apart on greased oven trays, sprinkle with seasoning. Bake in moderately hot oven about 15 minutes or until lightly browned; cool on trays.

Makes about 45.

ABOVE: Rich Blue Cheese and Poppyseed Biscuits.
RIGHT: Spicy Cheese Shapes.

PIZZA CHUNKS

½ cup (75g) plain flour
1½ cups (225g) self-raising flour
90g butter, chopped
½ cup (40g) grated parmesan cheese
½ cup (60g) seedless black olives, finely chopped
¼ cup (60ml) tomato paste
3 bacon rashers, finely chopped
2 tablespoons chopped fresh basil
1 egg yolk
1 tablespoon water, approximately

Add flours to large bowl, rub in butter, stir in cheese, olives, paste, bacon, basil, yolk and enough water to mix to a soft dough. Knead dough on lightly floured surface until smooth.

Divide dough into 3 portions, roll each portion between sheets of baking paper to 27cm x 32cm rectangle. Place each rectangle onto a greased oven tray. Bake in moderately hot oven about 15 minutes or until browned. Turn rectangles over, bake in moderately hot oven further 5 minutes or until browned underneath. Cool on wire racks; break into large pieces to serve.

BUTTERY CHEESE 'N' HAM BISCUITS

125g butter, chopped
1 cup (125g) finely grated tasty cheddar cheese
1½ tablespoons finely grated parmesan cheese
1 cup (150g) plain flour
70g ham, finely chopped
¼ teaspoon Tabasco sauce

Beat butter in small bowl with electric mixer until smooth. Stir in remaining ingredients. Roll rounded teaspoons of mixture into balls, place about 5cm apart on greased oven trays, flatten slightly with a floured fork. Bake in moderately hot oven about 20 minutes or until browned; cool on wire racks.

Makes about 35.

LEFT: Pizza Chunks.
ABOVE: Buttery Cheese 'n' Ham Biscuits.

Left: Basket from Barbara's Storehouse.

POPPYSEED BLISTERS

2 cups (300g) plain flour
60g butter, chopped
2 eggs, lightly beaten
2 tablespoons water, approximately
1 tablespoon milk
2 teaspoons sea salt
1 tablespoon poppyseeds

Add flour to medium bowl, rub in butter (or process flour and butter until mixture resembles coarse breadcrumbs). Add eggs and enough water to make ingredients cling together (or process until ingredients just come together). Knead lightly until smooth; refrigerate 30 minutes.

Divide dough into 2 portions. Roll each portion between sheets of baking paper until 2mm thick. Cut dough into 8cm rounds, place about 5cm apart on greased oven trays, brush with a little milk, sprinkle with combined salt and seeds. Bake in moderate oven about 15 minutes or until browned and blistered; cool on trays.

Makes about 30.

CHEESY OLIVE SESAME BISCUITS

Use chilli-flavoured or lemon-flavoured olives for a different taste.

1 cup (150g) plain flour
½ teaspoon baking powder
¼ cup (20g) rolled oats
90g butter, chopped
¾ cup (90g) finely grated tasty cheddar cheese
¼ cup (40g) seedless olives, chopped
1 tablespoon chopped fresh basil
1 egg yolk
1 tablespoon water, approximately
¼ cup (20g) grated parmesan cheese
1½ tablespoons sesame seeds

Combine flour, baking powder and oats in medium bowl, rub in butter. Stir in tasty cheese, olives and basil, add yolk and enough water to make ingredients cling together. Press dough into a ball, knead on lightly floured surface until smooth. Wrap in plastic wrap; refrigerate 30 minutes.

Roll dough between sheets of baking paper to 20cm x 30cm rectangle, trim edges. Cut rectangle into 5 x 4cm strips lengthways, then cut strips diagonally at 4cm intervals. Place shapes about 3cm apart on greased oven trays. Brush with a little water, sprinkle with combined parmesan cheese and seeds. Bake in moderately hot oven about 15 minutes or until lightly browned; cool on trays.

Makes about 30.

BELOW: Poppyseed Blisters.
RIGHT: Cheesy Olive Sesame Biscuits.

Below and right: China from Villeroy & Boch.

Butternut Cookies

Tim Tams

Golliwog

Shredded Wheatmeals

Scotch Fingers

Lattice

Granitas

Coconut Macaroons

BISCUITS

GLOSSARY

Here are some terms, names and alternatives to help everyone use and understand our recipes perfectly.

BACON RASHERS: bacon slices.

BAKING POWDER (double-acting baking powder): a raising agent consisting of an alkali and an acid. It is mostly made from cream of tartar and bicarbonate of soda in the proportions of 1 level teaspoon of cream of tartar to ½ level teaspoon bicarbonate of soda. This is equivalent to 2 teaspoons of baking powder.

BICARBONATE OF SODA: baking soda.

BISCUITS

Butternut Cookies: biscuits made from sugar, flour, rolled oats, butter, coconut and golden syrup.

Coconut Macaroons: made from coconut, egg white and cornflour.

Golliwog biscuits: un-iced biscuits made from flour, sugar, oil, cocoa, golden syrup and egg.

Granita biscuits: made from flour, sugar, oil, wheatmeal, butter, wheat flakes, golden syrup, egg and malt.

Lattice biscuits: flaky pastry biscuits made from flour, oil, sugar and milk powder.

Scotch Finger biscuits: made from flour, sugar, butter, oil, egg and condensed milk.

Shredded Wheatmeal biscuits: made from wheatmeal, flour, sugar, oil, bran and milk powder.

Tim Tams: chocolate biscuits coated in chocolate; made from chocolate, flour, sugar, oil, golden syrup, milk powder and cocoa.

BUTTER: we used salted butter in this book, but unsalted (also called sweet) butter can be used, if preferred; 125g is equal to 1 stick butter.

BUTTERMILK: is made by adding a culture to skim milk to give a slightly acidic flavour; skim milk can be substituted, if preferred.

CEREALS

Coco Pops: chocolate-flavoured puffed rice.

Corn Flakes: crisp flakes of corn.

Crunchy Nut Corn Flakes: crisp flakes of corn encrusted with nuts and honey.

Natural muesli: granola.

Oat bran: layer under the oat husk.

Oat bran

Wheat germ

Weet-Bix

Natural muesli

Toasted muesli

Rice Bubbles

Coco Pops

Corn Flakes

Crunchy Nut Corn Flakes

Rolled oats

Quick-cooking oats

CEREALS

Drinking chocolate

Cocoa

Carob powder

Milo

White Melts

Milk Melts

Choc Melts

Carob buttons

White chocolate

Milk chocolate

Dark chocolate

White Bits

Milk Bits

Choc Bits

Quick-cooking oats: need less cooking time than traditional oats.
Rice Bubbles: puffed rice.
Rolled oats: traditional oats.
Toasted muesli: crunchy granola.
Weet-Bix: wholewheat malted breakfast biscuit.
Wheat germ: flakes milled from the embryo of wheat.

CHOCOLATE AND CAROB
Carob buttons: chocolate substitute.
Carob powder: cocoa substitute.
Choc Bits: morsels; they do not melt during baking.
Choc Melts: for melting and moulding.
Cocoa: cocoa powder.
Dark chocolate: eating chocolate.
Drinking chocolate: sweetened cocoa powder.
Milk Bits: morsels; they do not melt during baking.
Milk chocolate: eating chocolate.
Milk Melts: for melting and moulding.
Milo: chocolate malted sweetened milk drink base.
White Bits: morsels; they do not melt during baking.
White chocolate: eating chocolate.
White Melts: for melting and moulding.

Flaked

Desiccated

Shredded

CONFECTIONERY
Almond Nougat bars: made from sugar, glucose, almonds, egg white and gelatine.
Cherry Ripe bars: made from chocolate, coconut, sugar, cherries, glucose and milk powder.
Chocolate-coated coffee beans: chocolate-coated roasted coffee beans.
Chocolate-coated sultanas: sultanas dipped in chocolate.
Coffee Eclairs: made from glucose, sugar, condensed milk, chocolate, oil and coffee extract.

Cherry Ripe bar

Yogurt-coated sultanas

Chocolate-coated sultanas

Violet Crumble bar

Maltesers

Toblerone bar

Licorice

Coffee Eclairs

Jersey Caramels

Chocolate-coated coffee beans

Marzipan

Popcorn

Puffed Corn

Milky Way bars

Almond Nougat bar

..kers bar

Mallow Bakes

Smarties

Milo bars

Marshmallows

Jersey Caramels: made from sugar, glucose, condensed milk, flour, oil and gelatine.

Licorice: made from flour, sugar, glucose, treacle, molasses and gelatine.

Mallow Bakes: coloured marshmallow pellets; made from sugar, glucose, cornflour and gelatine.

Maltesers: chocolates with crisp, light honeycomb centres; made from chocolate, glucose syrup, malt extract, milk powder, flour and sugar.

Marshmallows: pink and white; made from sugar, glucose, gelatine and cornflour.

Marzipan: made from sugar, almonds and glucose.

Milky Way bars: made from chocolate, sugar, glucose, malt, water, butter and egg white.

Milo bars: malt extract bars coated in milk chocolate.

Popcorn: a variety of corn that is sold as kernels for popping corn, or can be bought ready popped.

Puffed Corn: ready to eat snack made from whole yellow corn grains.

Smarties: made from chocolate, sugar and flour.

Snickers bars: made from chocolate, peanuts, glucose, sugar, milk powder, butter and egg white.

Toblerone bars: made from sugar, milk powder, cocoa, honey, almonds, glucose and egg white.

Violet Crumble bars: chocolate-dipped honeycomb; made from chocolate, sugar, glucose and gelatine.

Yogurt-coated sultanas: sultanas coated in powdered yogurt.

COPHA: a solid white shortening based on coconut oil. Kremelta and Palmin can be substituted.

CORNFLOUR: cornstarch.

CORNMEAL: ground corn (maize); similar to polenta but pale yellow and finer. One can be substituted for the other, but results will vary.

CORN SYRUP: an imported product. It is available in light or dark colour; either can be substituted for the other.

CREAM: fresh pouring cream; has a minimum fat content of 35 per cent.

Sour: a thick, commercially cultured, soured cream with 35 per cent fat.

Thickened (whipping): has a minimum fat content of 35 per cent, with the addition of a thickener.

CREME DE CACAO: chocolate liqueur.

CUSTARD POWDER: vanilla pudding mix.
ESSENCE: extract.

FLOUR

Plain: all-purpose.

Rice: flour made from ground rice.

Self-raising: substitute plain (all-purpose) flour and baking powder in the proportions of 1 cup (150g) plain flour to 2 level teaspoons baking powder.

Wholemeal plain: wholewheat flour without the addition of baking powder.

FRUIT

Fruit medley: combination of dried sultanas, apricots, apples, nectarines, peaches and pears.

Fruit mince: mince meat.

Mixed dried fruit: combination of sultanas, raisins, currants, peel and cherries.

Mixed peel: candied citrus peel.

Sultanas: golden raisins.

Sultanas

Mixed peel

Mixed dried fruit

Fruit mince

Fruit medley

FRANGELICO: a hazelnut-flavoured liqueur.

GELATINE: we used unflavoured powdered gelatine.

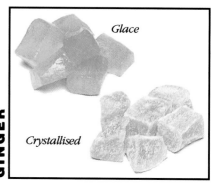

Glace

Crystallised

GLUCOSE SYRUP (liquid glucose): made from wheat starch.

GOLDEN SYRUP: maple, pancake syrup or honey can be substituted.

GRAND MARNIER: orange-flavoured liqueur.

HUNDREDS AND THOUSANDS: nonpareils.

INSTANT MALTED MILK POWDER: instant powdered product made from cows' milk, containing extracts of malted barley and other cereals.

JAM: conserve.

KAHLUA: coffee-flavoured liqueur.

MADEIRA CAKE: rich plain cake flavoured with lemon.

MAPLE-FLAVOURED SYRUP: golden/ pancake syrup; honey can be substituted.

MIXED SPICE: a blend of spices consisting of cinnamon, allspice and nutmeg.

MOLASSES: a thick, dark brown syrup, the residue of sugar refinement.

ORANGE FLOWER WATER: concentrated flavouring made from orange blossoms.

PIE APPLE: canned apples used for pie fillings.

PLAIN SWEET BISCUIT CRUMBS: crumbs made from plain, un-iced cookies.

PLAIN CAKE CRUMBS: crumbs made from plain, un-iced cake.

RICE PAPER: available from gourmet food shops and shops which specialise in Asian ingredients; it is edible.

RUM, DARK: we prefer to use an underproof (not overproof) rum.

SILVER CACHOUS: small, round, cake-decorating sweets, available in gold and other colours.

SPREADS

Chestnut: sweetened chestnut puree.

Lemon butter: curd or cheese.

Milky Way: white and dark chocolate hazelnut spread.

Nutella: chocolate hazelnut spread.

Tahini: ground sesame seeds.

SUGAR

Black: moist sugar with fine texture.

Brown: a soft, fine granulated sugar containing molasses.

Caster: fine granulated table sugar, also known as superfine.

Cinnamon sugar: combination of ground cinnamon and caster sugar.

Demerara: golden crystal sugar.

Icing sugar mixture: confectioners' or powdered sugar.

Raw: natural brown granulated sugar.

TIA MARIA: a coffee-flavoured liqueur.

VANILLA BEAN: can be used repeatedly, simply wash in warm water after use, dry well and store in airtight container.

VEGETABLE OIL: we used a polyunsaturated vegetable oil.

NUTS

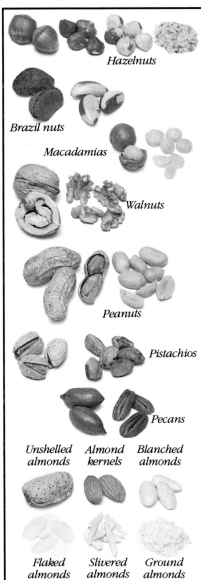

Hazelnuts

Brazil nuts

Macadamias

Walnuts

Peanuts

Pistachios

Pecans

Unshelled almonds   *Almond kernels*   *Blanched almonds*

Flaked almonds   *Slivered almonds*   *Ground almonds*

SEEDS

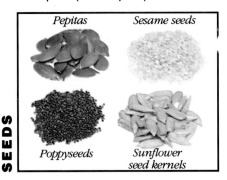

Pepitas   *Sesame seeds*

Poppyseeds   *Sunflower seed kernels*

Nutella

Lemon butter

Milky Way

Tahini

Chestnut puree

Raw sugar

Cinnamon sugar

Icing sugar mixture

Brown sugar

Demerara sugar

Caster sugar

Black sugar

■ Measure all ingredients accurately. When measuring dry ingredients, such as flour, gently tap the measuring cup to settle the flour, then use the back of a knife to make it level with the brim.

■ Use the correct-sized eggs and have all ingredients at room temperature.

■ Do not over-beat butter, sugar and egg mixtures. Over-beating will soften the mixture, which could cause biscuits to spread during baking.

■ Do not over-grease oven trays, or biscuits may burn underneath.

■ Use the correct cake pan or oven tray when baking biscuits and cookies. Use oven trays with little or no sides. If the sides are more than 1cm high, the heat cannot circulate properly to brown the biscuits.

■ Our oven temperatures and cooking times are only a guide, as every oven is different. Check manufacturer's instructions. You may need to adjust our cooking times a little.

■ As a guide, it is best to position biscuits and slices towards the top half of a gas oven and towards the lower half of an electric oven. In a fan-forced oven, the heat distribution should be even. Check manufacturer's instructions.

■ Several trays of biscuits can be baked in the oven at the same time, provided the trays do not touch the oven walls or the closed door. There must be space around each tray to allow the heat to circulate evenly. Don't be afraid to open the oven door to check if the biscuits are browning evenly. Turn the trays, if necessary. It is best to rotate trays half way during baking to ensure even browning. In a fan-forced oven, biscuits should brown and bake evenly without turning or rotating.

■ To test if biscuits and cookies are cooked: they should still feel slightly soft on the tray. Give them a gentle push with your finger; they should keep their shape, but loosen on the tray so they slip a little without breaking. Biscuits and cookies will become crisp on cooling.

WHAT DID I DO WRONG?

■ **Biscuits spread on tray:** incorrect measuring of ingredients; mixture too soft, usually due to over-beating; oven not hot enough.

■ **Biscuits too hard:** incorrect measuring of ingredients; biscuits overcooked; oven temperature too high.

■ **Biscuits too soft:** undercooked; not cooled in single layer on wire racks; not cooled completely before storing.

■ **Biscuits over-browned underneath:** incorrect measuring of ingredients, usually sugar, honey, golden syrup, etc.; oven tray over-greased; incorrect oven position; incorrect oven temperature.

STORAGE

■ Most biscuits and some slices keep well in an airtight container; creamy slices should, of course, be refrigerated.

■ Cool biscuits completely before storing.

■ Biscuits which are filled with jam or icing are best eaten the same day; fillings and icings will soften the biscuits.

■ To crisp soft, un-iced or unfilled biscuits, place on oven tray in single layer, bake in moderate oven about 5 minutes.

TOASTING NUTS & COCONUT

■ Toasting brings out the flavour in nuts and coconut. Spread nuts or coconut evenly onto oven tray, bake in moderate oven about 5 minutes or grill until browned. Shake tray and stir nuts occasionally during toasting. Alternatively, spread nuts or coconut evenly in dry, heavy-based frying pan, stir over medium heat until browned.

MICROWAVE SHORTCUTS

Make use of the microwave oven to speed up preparations.

■ To melt butter, simply microwave on HIGH in a microwave-proof bowl, then add the remaining ingredients. Melting time will depend on the butter quantity.

■ Some melt-and-mix recipes which are started in a saucepan can be started in a microwave-proof bowl on HIGH in the microwave oven. The time will depend on the quantity.

■ To melt chocolate, break up blocks or spread Melts in a single layer on a microwave-safe plate, microwave on HIGH until chocolate is soft. Remember, it will still hold most of its shape even when melted. The time it takes to melt will depend on the oven and the amount; start checking after 30 seconds. Never allow water to touch melted chocolate or it will be ruined.

■ To dissolve gelatine, place the gelatine and the specified liquid in a microwave-proof jug or cup, microwave on HIGH until dissolved. The time it takes depends on the quantity; start with about 20 seconds.

QUICK CONVERSION GUIDE

Wherever you live in the world you can use our recipes with the help of our easy-to-follow conversions for all your cooking needs. These conversions are approximate only. The difference between the exact and approximate conversions of liquid and dry measures amounts to only a teaspoon or two, and will not make any difference to your cooking results.

MEASURING EQUIPMENT

The difference between measuring cups internationally is minimal within 2 or 3 teaspoons' difference. (For the record, 1 Australian metric measuring cup will hold approximately 250ml.) The most accurate way of measuring dry ingredients is to weigh them. When measuring liquids use a clear glass or plastic jug with metric markings.

If you would like the measuring cups and spoons as used in our Test Kitchen, turn to page 128 for details and the order coupon. In this book we use metric measuring cups and spoons approved by Standards Australia.

● a graduated set of four cups for measuring dry ingredients; the sizes are marked on the cups.
● a graduated set of four spoons for measuring dry and liquid ingredients; the amounts are marked on the spoons.
● 1 TEASPOON: 5ml.
● 1 TABLESPOON: 20ml.

NOTE: NZ, CANADA, USA AND UK ALL USE 15ml TABLESPOONS.
ALL CUP AND SPOON MEASUREMENTS ARE LEVEL UNLESS OTHERWISE SPECIFIED.

DRY MEASURES

METRIC	IMPERIAL
15g	½oz
30g	1oz
60g	2oz
90g	3oz
125g	4oz (¼lb)
155g	5oz
185g	6oz
220g	7oz
250g	8oz (½lb)
280g	9oz
315g	10oz
345g	11oz
375g	12oz (¾lb)
410g	13oz
440g	14oz
470g	15oz
500g	16oz (1lb)
750g	24oz (1½lb)
1kg	32oz (2lb)

LIQUID MEASURES

METRIC	IMPERIAL
30ml	1 fluid oz
60ml	2 fluid oz
100ml	3 fluid oz
125ml	4 fluid oz
150ml	5 fluid oz (¼ pint/1 gill)
190ml	6 fluid oz
250ml	8 fluid oz
300ml	10 fluid oz (½ pint)
500ml	16 fluid oz
600ml	20 fluid oz (1 pint)
1000ml (1 litre)	1¾ pints

WE USED LARGE EGGS WITH AN AVERAGE WEIGHT OF 60g.

USE BUTTER AND EGGS AT ROOM TEMPERATURE FOR BEST RESULTS.

HELPFUL MEASURES

METRIC	IMPERIAL
3mm	⅛in
6mm	¼in
1cm	½in
2cm	¾in
2.5cm	1in
5cm	2in
6cm	2½in
8cm	3in
10cm	4in
13cm	5in
15cm	6in
18cm	7in
20cm	8in
23cm	9in
25cm	10in
28cm	11in
30cm	12in (1ft)

HOW TO MEASURE

When using the graduated metric measuring cups, it is important to shake the dry ingredients loosely into the required cup. Do not tap the cup on the bench, or pack the ingredients into the cup unless otherwise directed. Level top of cup with knife. When using graduated metric measuring spoons, level top of spoon with knife. When measuring liquids in the jug, place jug on flat surface, check for accuracy at eye level.

OVEN TEMPERATURES

These oven temperatures are only a guide; we've given you the lower degree of heat. Always check the manufacturer's manual.

	C° (Celsius)	F° (Fahrenheit)	Gas Mark
Very slow	120	250	1
Slow	150	300	2
Moderately slow	160	325	3
Moderate	180 – 190	350 – 375	4
Moderately hot	200 – 210	400 – 425	5
Hot	220 – 230	450 – 475	6
Very hot	240 – 250	500 – 525	7

TWO GREAT OFFERS FROM THE AWW HOME LIBRARY

Here's the perfect way to keep your Home Library books in order, clean and within easy reach. More than a dozen books fit into this smart silver grey vinyl folder. PRICE: Australia $9.95; elsewhere $19.95; prices include postage and handling. To order your holder, see the details below.

All recipes in the AWW Home Library are created using Australia's unique system of metric cups and spoons. While it is relatively easy for overseas readers to make any minor conversions required, it is easier still to own this durable set of Australian cups and spoons (photographed). PRICE : Australia: $5.95; New Zealand: $A8.00; elsewhere: $A9.95; prices include postage & handling.
This offer is available in all countries.

TO ORDER YOUR METRIC MEASURING SET OR BOOK HOLDER:

PHONE: Have your credit card details ready. **Sydney:** (02) 260 0035; **elsewhere in Australia:** 008 252 515 (free call, Mon-Fri, 9am-5pm) or *FAX* your order to (02) 267 4363 or *MAIL* your order by photocopying or cutting out and completing the coupon below.

PAYMENT: **Australian residents:** We accept the credit cards listed, money orders and cheques. **Overseas residents:** We accept the credit cards listed, drafts in $A drawn on an Australian bank, also English, New Zealand and U.S. cheques in the currency of the country of issue.
Credit card charges are at the exchange rate current at the time of payment.

Please photocopy and complete coupon and fax or send to:
AWW Home Library Reader Offer, ACP Direct, PO Box 7036, Sydney 2001.